Tell Me About Yourself

Tell Me About Yourself

Personal Branding and Social Media Recruiting in the Brave New Online World

Stavros Papakonstantinidis

BEP BUSINESS EXPERT PRESS

First published in 2019 by
Business Expert Press, LLC
222 East 46th Street, New York, NY 10017
www.businessexpertpress.com

ISBN-13: 978-1-63157-523-5 (paperback)
ISBN-13: 978-1-63157-524-2 (e-book)

Business Expert Press Digital and Social Media Marketing
and Advertising Collection

Collection ISSN: 2333-8822 (print)
Collection ISSN: 2333-8830 (electronic)

Cover and interior design by S4Carlisle Publishing Services Private Ltd., Chennai, India

First edition: 2019

10 9 8 7 6 5 4 3 2 1

Printed in the United States of America.

To Nikoleta, Konstantina^2 and Leonidas^2

Abstract

What is branding and what makes people passionate about it? How can people develop and maintain a unique online persona? Who are the current trendsetters in personal branding? What makes social recruiting so important in today's business world? Why is it necessary to set up a personal brand strategy early on? What are some future trends in social recruiting and personal branding?

The rules of recruitment and job searching have undoubtedly changed as a new breed of concept workers enters the global workforce. Today, we are witnessing the emergence of a non–age-specific generation of professionals who are exposed to ubiquitous digital technology and seek a more impactful job, an easygoing life, and a safe future.

We could call them Gen X, Gen Y, millennials, or digital natives. The book *Tell Me About Yourself: Personal Branding and Social Media Recruiting in the Brave New Online World* introduces the term *social natives* to explain why these individuals are unique. They share bits of information at a rapid pace and are capable of processing projects parallelly. They live on their phones and are in favor of graphics over text. Social natives prefer to read on smart devices, get the news through their timelines, and function better when they join networks. Social natives started realizing the importance of personal branding as a means to stand out from the crowd and attract viewers, followers, advertisers, and, eventually, employers.

Social natives are now looking for jobs in various ways that did not exist five years ago. Emerging technologies, artificial intelligence business tools, wearable gadgets, and social media platforms such as LinkedIn, Facebook, BranchOut, Twitter Jobs, Glassdoor, Viadeo, XING, and Bayt, define today's fast-paced professional world. Social natives use blogs, podcasts, online bios, video résumés, images, selfies, recommendations, and endorsements to publicly demonstrate their skills.

Such online technologies facilitate the recruitment and selection of job candidates via the integration of intelligent software applications in the web-based talent search. The breadth and depth of information increase as HR managers and recruiters embrace new digital tools and platforms. Tomorrow's successful organizations use Big Data, business intelligence, and People Analytics, as well as a plethora of social media screening tools to recruit and retain great talents.

This book will help you understand how social media in professional recruitment works. It will also inspire you through various success stories to take personal branding toward professional career development seriously. Finally, this book examines social nativity as a social phenomenon and presents the latest trends in career development and social recruiting.

Keywords

human resources management; online personas; personal branding; recruiting firms; social influencers; social media; social networking; social recruitment

Contents

Preface .... *xi*

Setting the Scene .... *xxix*

Chapter 1   From Brands to Humans 1

Chapter 2   Personal Branding 15

Chapter 3   The Social Natives 31

Chapter 4   Recruiting in the Brave New Online Social World 49

Chapter 5   The Brand New Me 61

Chapter 6   The Brave New Online World 75

References *87*

About the Author *95*

Index *97*

Preface

This section at a glance:
- Tell me about yourself
- Opportunities in a brave new online world
- A brief history of the Internet
- The development of social recruiting
- The era of personal branding
- The significance of personal branding
- Reasons to read this book
- The questions this book aims to answer

Tell Me About Yourself

It is one of the most commonly asked questions during job interviews. Recruiters, hiring managers, or business owners often kick off interviews with a simple and straightforward question. Is it though? You can start a friendly conversation with people you would like to meet or catch up with. When the "tell me about yourself" is asked during a job interview, it can make you sweat. What should you say to demonstrate that you are the perfect candidate for the job? How much of yourself should you expose to build rapport with the interviewers and get them to trust you? What do they want to hear from you?

In a question like this, the recruiter does not want to hear your life story. The interviewer wants to know how your achievements relate to the job for which you have applied. Your answer will allow you to demonstrate how much you know about the available job position and the company's values. It will also provide you with the opportunity to highlight your skills, experience, and personality. What is more important for you? How are you going to start answering such question? Will you repeat what they already know by reading your resume? Will you try to surprise them? Remember that the hiring manager wants to hear what makes you the best candidate for a job. And because usually hiring managers kick off the job interview by asking this question, it can help you find the right words to make a great first impression. In other words, the "tell me about yourself" question allows you to brand yourself and bravely sell it most impressively.

Brand and sell yourself? You may wonder, "Why should I brand myself?" Personal branding is to publicly answer the "tell me about yourself" question using social media. This book is about personal branding in the digital era. In Aldous Huxley's (1932) famous dystopian novel, *The Brave New World*, Hatchery's director and one of his assistants are showing to a group of young boys the developments in reproductive technology, hypnopedia (sleep-learning), psychological manipulation, and classical conditioning as elements that will profoundly change our society.

Of course, this book is not about Huxley's world. This book is about our efforts to stand out in today's professional world and meet with its demands to bravely expose ourselves on the Internet. Whether we consider it ethical to do so or not, our brave new online world expects us to function as brands that are ready to compete in a competitive and adaptive marketing landscape.

Opportunities in the Brave New Online World

The Internet has impacted the way we communicate, share information, and share and exchange messages. The Internet is not merely a new channel of communication. Instead, it is a unique environment in which people interact, work, and learn. It has affected a broad spectrum of our daily activities. The Internet is the context and not merely a tool with limitless content (Hooley 2012). The Internet has raised social implications, and it is critical for scholars to explain computer-mediated communication.

The Internet brought to people's lives a profound change in the way they search for information and share intelligence. There are over 40,000 search queries posted on Google every second. This translates into over 3.5 billion daily searches and 1.2 trillion searches per year worldwide (Internetlivestats.com 2017). The Internet has become ubiquitous.

Personal computers or laptops are no longer the only devices that allow people to connect online. They used to be, but not anymore. Users can access the web using mobile devices as well. New technologies emerge regularly, such as the Internet of Things (IoT), which integrates online access with purchase of personal accessories (glasses, watches, jackets, etc.) and domestic appliances (fridges, closets, coffeemakers, etc.; Meola 2018). The dynamic changes due to emerging technologies in the Internet-driven social sphere or the online world are becoming increasingly visible and recognizable. How people organize their data (e.g., using cloud computing), how they ask search engines for anything, including wondering "Who they are" or "What to vote," and the kind of other personal search queries they post have changed completely. There are more than 1 billion search queries on Google every day. Google reports that "15 percent of the searches it sees every day have never been seen before."

In 2010, Google introduced the "autocomplete" feature. All you have to do is to write the first few letters of a word, the Google search engine completes the rest and does the search. It suggests possible words or phrases that might apply to your search based on your frequently used past search queries. This has led to autocomplete feature yielding some pretty funny results. For instance, the classic "what would happen if . . ." query is able to bring the most unexpected results such as "what would happen if the sun exploded?," "What would happen if there was no moon?," and so on. People ask Google to find them a job, to help them with their relationships, or to assist them with changing their lives. Also, people ask Google for advice on their personal branding.

The Internet profoundly affected almost every aspect of social life. With the use of social media, the lines between private and public life have blurred. Nowadays, it is quite common for social media–savvy users to expose their personal moments on platforms like Facebook, Instagram, or Snapchat. Their daily schedule is posted online, so their followers know where they are, what they are doing, what they like, and how their life looks like. They see no problem with it. Sometimes they do not have to post their actual experience when they can fake one. Molloy (2017) reports that a Moscow-based company specializes in renting out a grounded private jet for professional Instagram photo shoots for those social media users who wish to satisfy their vanity to get more likes from their followers.

An interesting and somewhat controversial story of personal branding is that of Dan "Blitz" Bilzerian, who is commonly known as the King of Instagram. He demonstrates an enticing and outrageous lifestyle to over 20 million Instagram followers as a playboy and professional poker player who hangs out with celebrities and top models. In Ayres' (2017) story on *GQ Magazine*, which is titled "The truth about Dan Bilzerian," the reporter questions Bilzerian's true identity and origin of wealth. This might as well be another story of an Internet persona who managed to take full advantage of the existing opportunities in our brave new online world.

Do we trust the Internet for everything? The report, "Future of Truth and Misinformation Online," reveals that Americans are confused about what will happen in the future information environment; 51 percent support the statement that the information environment will not improve, whereas 49 percent say the information environment would become more trustworthy (Anderson and Rainie 2017). People seem to trust social media as a more reliable source of information than traditional media (Ingram 2016). College students use Wikipedia and other free online sources as educational tools in their academic life. People trust crowd-sourced readers such as Yelp.com and online platforms such as Booking.com or Tripadvisor.com for reviews and peer recommendations before they complete their digital customer journey and decide (Edelman and Singer 2015).

People use the Internet for entertainment purposes as well. Online games, music streaming applications, contact-less purchases, online wallets, web torrents are all examples of online social entertainment behaviors. With the rapid proliferation of e-commerce, scholars start examining the implications of the so-called online currency, Bitcoin, especially whether or not it can contribute to the actual economy (Holmes 2018). The new online world is full of surprises and opportunities for people to stand out from the crowd and make an impact. How do companies take advantage of the new online environment?

Employer branding, CEO branding, social and mobile recruiting, millennials' recruiting, talent acquisition and retention, and trust and transparency are among the most discussed trends and topics in business.

Glassdoor for Employers (2017) published a statistical guide for recruiters collecting several recruiting and employee engagement statistics from well-known trend watchers like Deloitte and Gallup. The findings provided in the following demonstrate what drives jobseekers and employees to apply for a job or cultivate a sense of meaning within their current job environment.

About 66 percent of millennials expect to leave their organization by 2020. Source: Deloitte, *Millennial Survey 2016*, January 2016.

- About 39 percent of women say the reputation or brand of the company is "very important" to them when considering a job move. A somewhat smaller percentage of women (32 percent) say the same about the company's cause. For 33 percent of men, the company's brand is "very important," but only 22 percent feel the same about the company's cause. Source: Gallup, *Women in America*, October 2016.
- As much as 72 percent of CEOs are concerned about the availability of key skills. Source: PwC, *19th Annual Global CEO Survey*, 2016.
- Organizations that invest in employer branding are three times more likely to make a quality hire. Source: Brandon Hall, *The True Cost of a Bad Hire*, September 2015.
- Organizations that invest in a strong candidate experience improve their quality of hires by 70 percent. Source: Brandon Hall, *The True Cost of a Bad Hire*, September 2015.
- Glassdoor users report they use an average of 7.6 job sites during their job search. Source: *Glassdoor.com Site Survey*, January 2016.
- About 10 percent of the more difficult job interview process is associated with 2.6 percent higher employee satisfaction later on. Source: *Glassdoor Economic Research*, October 2015.

(Glassdoor for Employers 2017)

A Brief History of the Internet

The rapid proliferation of the Internet in the early 1990s raised questions in the global business environment. The World Wide Web as a new communication platform was expected to enhance and facilitate considerable knowledge of humanity, businesses, cultures, and languages. The first version of the Internet was primarily a nondynamic representation of information, published by the few users who had access and the recourses to maintain a website. The dotcom bubble collapse in 2001 signified the eruption of Web 2.0 as the more interactive version with user-generated content, which was promising radical changes in the way people use the World Wide Web. A more interactive version of the network now offers unlimited access for all, facilitating the emergence of new tools and modes that have radically altered how business communications are carried out. Nevertheless, we see rigorous academic debate among those, including sociologists and academicians, who are opposed to the broader notion of the Internet as the *sine qua non* to human interaction.

Amid the sudden transformation of global social processes, the Internet has turned out to be a mixed blessing. The Internet functions as an active channel of communication, which can facilitate compassionate and empathic exchanges across cultures and languages. It signifies the birth of alternative occupational opportunities at a time when traditional organizations seem unable to recruit and retain the best minds. On the other hand, the Internet may also amplify cultural differences as to how people seek and apply for jobs. As the influence of traditional recruiting channels will be reduced or even vanish, the gap between computer literates and computer illiterates will be more evident than ever before (Manafy and Gautschi 2011).

The emergence of online Social Networking Sites (SNS) ushered in a massive shift in today's labor market. Human Resources Management (HRM) models have transformed the scope of employee–employer relationships and ushered radical changes in how people function in a range of spheres, including in interpersonal, intercultural, organizational, and mass communication contexts. Millions are logging into SNS every day, making it hard to calculate with precision the total number of users and the average time they spend on the Internet.

This book looks at how social media is shaping a new reality in (HRM) processes and the experiences of candidates involved in recruitment. Until recently, the process of seeking a job or recruiting the best minds made companies either to post their job vacancy on the corporate website or to post an expensive job advert on the newspapers and online job boards (i.e., Monster.com). Newer job-posting sites such as Indeed. com and SimplyHired.com interface with LinkedIn to perform abductive searches of significant job boards all around the globe, thereby providing users with a natural, one-stop search.

Traditional recruiting practices will likely continue to decline in global influence, as social networking websites and other forms of online HRM business process services are available. Social media already plays a major role in recruitment and job search. The social media statistics as presented below are fascinating:

- About 75 percent of male Internet users as well as 83 percent of female Internet users are on Facebook.
- According to recode, 44 percent of teenagers asked to choose one social network if "trapped on a deserted island" chose Snapchat, ahead of Instagram (24 percent) and Facebook (14 percent).
- Female Internet users are more likely to use Instagram than men, at 38 percent versus 26 percent.
- As much as 29 percent of Internet users with college degrees use Twitter, compared to 20 percent with high school degrees or less.
- About 81 percent of millennials check Twitter at least once per day.
- About 91 percent of social media users are accessing social channels via mobile devices.
- About 22 percent of the world's total population uses Facebook.
- LinkedIn boasts more than 530 million user profiles.
- On any given day, Snapchat reaches 41 percent of 18- to 34-year-olds in the United States.
- YouTube overall and even YouTube on mobile alone reach more 18- to 34-year-olds and 18- to 49-year-olds than any cable network in the United States.

(*continued*)

- Facebook continues to be the most widely used social media platform, with 79 percent of American Internet users.
- Instagram received the silver medal with 32 percent of users, with Pinterest coming in a close third with 31 percent, and LinkedIn and Twitter at 29 percent and 24 percent, respectively.
- The average LinkedIn user spends 17 minutes on the site per month.
- As much as 51 percent of Instagram users access the platform daily, and 35 percent say they look at the platform several times a day.
- Almost 80 percent of time spent on social media platforms happens on mobile.
- Katy Perry has the most worldwide Twitter followers, at 94.65 million.
- Over 400 million snaps are shared on Snapchat per day, and almost 9,000 photos are shared every second.
- Just 10,000 YouTube videos have generated more than 1 billion views.
- More than half of all YouTube views are on mobile devices.
- Instagram earns $595 million in mobile ad revenue per year, a rapidly increasing number.
- About 100 million hours of video content are watched on Facebook daily.
- As much as 88 percent of businesses with more than 100 employees use Twitter for marketing purposes.
- The user-submitted YouTube video with the most views is "Charlie bit my finger" with over 845 million views.
- Pizza is the most widely Instagrammed food, directly ahead of steak and sushi.
- Blogging continues to grow, with over 409 million people viewing more than 23.6 billion pages each month on WordPress alone.

(Lister 2018)

The Development of Social Recruiting

There are currently 467 million LinkedIn users. Of those, 106 million are actively using LinkedIn monthly, whereas 40 percent of users use LinkedIn daily, following at least one of the 1.5 million professional groups on LinkedIn (Domkundwar 2017). LinkedIn is not the only professional networking website. Listed in alphabetical order are the names of several online communities and networking sites where job searchers and recruiters meet and exchange ideas: AngelList, Bark, Bayt, Beyond, BranchOut, Data.com Connect, Doostang, EFactor, Jobcase, LocalsNetworking, Lunchmeet, Marketbase, Meetup, Opportunity, PartnerUp, Plaxo, Sumry, Twylah, VisualCV, Xing, and Zerply.

Although the numbers mentioned previously are still not matching the vast number of professional résumés posted on job sites, soon social media will outnumber anything else in the area of recruitment. The reason for SNS' rapid and constant growth is the fact that they are easier to use and, most important, free of charge. Although SNS first promised to provide people a social space to meet and chat, they have turned into a significant boon for HRM specialists (Gibbs, MacDonald, and MacKay 2015).

Social media is even described as the panacea of communication and interactivity among the members in the business world. The option by Facebook to classify our friends based on occupation and schools, as well as the various professional applications of LinkedIn, the online reviews on Glassdoor, and the growing use of Twitter job feeds, shows that competition is high and multifaceted. What started as a social trend is currently shaping the future of business performance. This transformation begins with recruiting the most talented human capital. Companies now look for highly qualified recruits, as career seekers are actively using the SNS.

Employers no longer need to use the paid services of an HRM firm for the first stage of the recruitment process. Until now, HR managers and recruiters had to review CVs mailed directly to the company's offices or posted online on a job board. Then they would have to screen the information and decide from the two- to three-page profile which candidate was to qualify for the next round of the recruiting process. With the use of social networks, jobseekers have already uploaded online their information as well as academic and professional qualifications. Upon hearing from prospective employers, candidates may also submit their response online. Professional recommendations offer ready access for HRM or colleague review. Also, candidates who are building their online personal and professional profiles can uncover the full identity that will allow them to pursue their dream career.

Employers now look for candidates with extended networks of interest. Profiles enriched with their pictures, friends, thoughts, affiliations, and group memberships stand to perform better. A person's online profile on LinkedIn offers information in greater depth about his/her professional qualifications than a static piece of paper, and it also provides the recruiter an opportunity to assess a candidate's social profile in unguarded moments.

Even though SNS are poised to completely take over the hiring process, there are still enough number of candidates who do not have an active presence in social media. So, how can HRM address the needs of those career seekers who are not using new social networks to look for career opportunities? What are the ethical issues raised by the growing demand for people to share their personal thoughts, news, and highlights publicly? In what way does HRM tackle the growing interest of corporates to overly use social media to recruit best candidates to fill vacant positions?

It is perhaps effectively argued that continuity in the business environment remains one of the critical factors affecting the functioning of any organization. The "people factor" establishes a baseline competency criterion for the health of an entity, and social recruiting presentation is no exception. Recruitment is a two-way street. HRM professionals acknowledge that to attract and retain the most desirable candidates, excellence in organizational performance must be evidenced in marketing. Where compensation and professional benefits to employment are not availed, recruitment may fail. Communication of current market offerings in the profession is destined to be a foundation for the survival of any business in turbulent environments.

Unconventional elements in the HRM environment are now at the center of strategic planning in recruitment campaigns. Social media marketing arrived on the scene during a period of global change in business. Universal, cost-effective solutions, afforded by access to social media–based marketing, initiated a more complex, yet vital, arena of professional identity for professionals; social media(ted) character is a quality taken for granted in recruitment relations (Gibbs, MacDonald, and MacKay 2015).

The rapid adoption of social media by the professional world in communications, marketing, and HRM developed the concept of social recruiting. As more companies look online to hire the best talent, the online users have begun to adapt themselves to the new online environment and its demands. Users are increasingly seeing themselves as brands and, thus, recognize the need to communicate publicly and digitally their skills and expertise. Hence, the era of personal branding has just begun.

The Era of Personal Branding

In traditional marketing, branding is much more than a logo and a slogan. In his blog, Dempsey (2017) writes: "a brand is a feeling and emotion, something much deeper than just the visual appeal." Marketers work toward building and maintaining their product's brand identity as how customers should perceive it (Labrecque, Markos, and Milne 2011). A well-established commercial brand expresses its core values, purpose, and messages to the public.

Think of brands like Nike, Red Bull, Apple, or BMW. What all those brands have in common is their strong perceived impression. In other words, it is about creating brand equity or brand premium. The moment you see a brand or a logo, for example, Nike's swoosh logo, you start thinking about sports, energy, innovation, and reliability, depending on the brand or the logo that you see. How does this happen? This is because well-established brands have personalities. They have a sharp and bright soul. Just as commercial brands, humans can also develop a publicly perceived impression. If brands can communicate their character, so can humans.

Personal branding is a rather new term and new concept in literature. A simple comparison on Google Trends reveals that until 2010, "personal branding" was not commonly used and searched as much as the terms "self-presentation" and "self-promotion" were. Since 2010, personal branding has been widely discussed and searched on Google, more than any other similar terms. Labrecque, Markos, and Milne (2011) argue that through branding individuals are able to capture and promote their strengths and unique characteristics.

Personal branding is a

process by which individuals and entrepreneurs differentiate themselves and stand out from a crowd by identifying and articulating their unique value proposition, whether professional or personal and then leverage it across platforms with a consistent message and image to achieve a specific goal. (Schawbel 2010, p. 6)

Let's simplify these definitions. Social media allows individuals to openly and directly communicate with each other online. Consequently, several online users are able to establish several communities of interest that offer them a chance to stand out and increase their popularity.

Just as a jobseeker would craft the perfect answer to the interview question "tell me about yourself," individuals who want to develop their online personal brand should ask themselves what they stand for and what makes them unique. As marketing experts test and cultivate their brands to look and behave like humans, individuals should do the same. They should identify their unique value proposition and find the one thing that they do exceptionally well. Whether individuals sing, dance, dress, or play video games, their primary concern should be to identify their audience and get to know them well.

Personal branding is not merely about creating and posting online a resume to promote profile visibility for organizations looking to hire. People who are into self-branding should think of themselves as brands in a highly competitive market (Barnett 2010). These personal brands should always project qualities that make them appear creative, unique, and exciting to their followers and subscribers, in other words, qualities none too easy or common to come by. Personal branding includes a representation of people's personalities through a variety of media. The pattern is clear. Keep your followers happy and entertained. This will bring you more viewers and will increase your popularity. This will generate more leads and revenue. Of course, this is all in theory. It is not that simple in practice because not all can succeed in creating a long-lasting personal brand.

Is personal branding only for those select few who want to share their uniqueness with their online followers? Of course not. Many online users need to realize that most probably they are already involved in personal branding, even if they are not aware of it. This is due to the power of search engines such as Google, Yahoo!, and Bing. Once someone's name appears on the Internet, they become a keyword. Search engines can bring up your name if someone types it into a search engine bar. No matter what individuals aim to establish or find any kind of occupation, carefully crafting and protecting your personal brand and digital reputation has become a necessity.

The Significance of Personal Branding

Personal branding is a significant aspect of job candidates' planning for their careers (Friedman 2015). The job market nowadays is more competitive and limited than ever. Companies often outsource their operations or recruit people from a global pool of candidates via the Internet. A job candidate with a strong and competitive personal brand has fewer chances to run out of professional options. Also, personal branding on social media might either strengthen or weaken a candidate's profile depending on the kind of information that appears online.

A recent study conducted by Jobvite reveals that a growing number of companies adopt social recruiting strategies and modern recruiters engage in social screening by searching for future employees (Van Nuys 2017). In 2006 during the recruitment process, only 11 percent of employers were assessing their job applicants' digital footprint (search results and social media), but in 2017 almost 70 percent of recruiters used social media and search engines for the same reason (CareerBuilder 2017). The same study revealed that 50 percent of employers used all major search engines (Google, Yahoo!, Bing) and major SNS (Facebook, LinkedIn, Twitter, Instagram) to assure that the job applicant has a professional online profile, and 37 percent also checked what other online users, friends, and followers are posting about the applicant. As much as 24 percent of the surveyed employers answered that they regularly checked online for a specific candidate's profile to determine whether or not to reject his/her application.

The primary task for job candidates is to market themselves by using the power of digital tools to their advantage (Labrecque, Markos, and Milne 2011). Hence, jobseekers should become more aware of the opportunities provided by personal branding and offer anything that protects their online reputation. In today's environment, our own brand and digital reputation accompany us in anything we do. Even in social events, for example, meeting others at a party, people no longer share their personal phone numbers. All they do is to connect on social media and start checking each other's profiles.

It is no secret that companies are reviewing candidates' social media accounts and they are looking for information to either hire or reject a person based on his/her online content. Therefore, our personal brand is probably the most important asset to building and maintaining our career. Jobseekers are not helpless. If employers can screen online the jobseekers' profiles to decide whether to hire or reject them, so can jobseekers do the same. Jobseekers can decide whether they want to work for a company or not based on information available online about that company. Also, people can take advantage of personal branding to increase their popularity and impact on society. There are too many success stories of individuals who managed to build a strong personal brand online and developed their own business. This book presents some of the most recent success stories to inspire and encourage people to take their "personal brand" seriously. So, what do you think? Is a book on personal branding worth reading?

Reasons to Read This Book

Instead of stating vague reasons to read the book, the author chose to present important statistics collected by Erskine (2016) from various online sources. The statistics posted on Entrepreneur provide evidence why people should get involved in developing and maintaining their own brand.

The Power of Employees' Personal Brands

- When brand messages are shared by employees on social media, they get 561 percent more reach than the same messages shared by the brand's social media channels.
- Brand messages are reshared 24 times more frequently when posted by an employee versus the brand's social media channels.
- On average, employees have 10 times more followers than their company's social media accounts.
- Content shared by employees receives eight times more engagement than content shared by brand channels.

Personal Branding Helps Sales and Marketing

- Leads developed through employees' social media activities convert seven times more frequently than other leads.
- Sales reps who use social media as part of their sales techniques outsell 78 percent of their peers.
- As much as 92 percent of people trust recommendations from other individuals (even if they don't know them) over brands.
- Marketers, who prioritize blogging, are 13 times more likely to enjoy positive ROI.

The Power of Social Media in Recruiting

- Employees at companies that invest in personal branding initiatives are 27 percent more likely to feel optimistic about their company's future; 20 percent are more likely to stay with their company, and 40 percent are more likely to believe their company is more competitive.
- As much as 95 percent of the recruiters believe that the job market will remain or become more competitive. If you don't stand out online, your competition will.
- About 75 percent of HR departments are required to search job applicants online.
- About 85 percent of U.S. recruiters and HR professionals say that an employee's online reputation influences their hiring

(*continued*)

decisions at least to some extent. Nearly half say that a strong
online reputation influences their decisions to a great extent.

- About 70 percent of U.S. recruiters and HR professionals have
rejected candidates based on information they found online.
- Of all executive recruiters, 90 percent say they conduct online
research of potential candidates.

Personal Branding for Online Reputation Management

- Reputation damage is the number one risk/concern for business
executives around the world, and 88 percent of them say they are
explicitly focusing on reputation risk as a key business challenge.
- Of all executives, 87 percent rate reputation risk as more important or much more important than other strategic risks their
companies are facing.
- Of respondents who experienced a reputation risk event,
41 percent say the loss of revenue was the biggest impact.

Growing Your Business with Personal Branding

- Out of all business decision-makers, 84 percent start their buying process with a referral. Google is the very first place people
look for a referral.
- Of all Internet users, 65 percent see online search as the most
trusted source of information about people and companies.
- About 53 percent of decision-makers have eliminated a vendor
from consideration based on information they did or did not
find about an employee online.

Erskine (2016)

The Questions This Book Aims to Answer

It is not easy to make promises. Things are changing, and we should adapt
to the new personal and professional conditions. This book aims to inspire
you and make you more aware of your own brand. The following questions
aim to help you develop a clearer understanding of the scope of this book.

1. What is branding?
2. What makes people passionate about branding?
3. What is personal branding?
4. How can you develop and maintain a strong personal brand?
5. Who are the current trendsetters in personal branding?
6. What makes social natives unique?
7. What should we know about social recruiting and social screening?
8. Why is it necessary to set up your personal brand strategy early on?
9. What are the future trends in social recruiting and personal branding?
10. What should organizations need to know about the brave new online world?

In the following chapters, this book discusses real-life stories and business practices to explain the concept of personal branding. The target audiences of the book are social media enthusiasts, college students, job-seekers, hiring managers, job recruiters, HR practitioners, digital marketing consultants, and entrepreneurs. The next section provides a brief description of each chapter to set the scene.

Setting the Scene

Chapter 1 introduces the concept of branding. It starts with a discussion on consumer brands and ends with a discussion on personal brands. It explains the evolution of branding over the years, from the typical notion about branding being merely logos, colors, and fonts to be the heart and soul of organizations. Marketing has become more emotional, and as such, this chapter discusses the four passions of branding.

Chapter 2 focuses on the importance of personal branding. This chapter includes definitions of terms and synonyms regarding personal branding. This chapter offers a historical background to how personal branding evolved with the use of technology and social media. It discusses the concept of online social entertainment and its impact on how people communicate, share information, and enjoy their time. Finally, the chapter provides the readers with suggestions about how to set up their brand and explains what makes a personal brand successful.

Chapter 3 explains the terms *social natives* and *hashtag generation*. This chapter provides a theoretical background on human behavior describing how the *digital natives* who were born and raised in the technological era have become social natives who live and breathe in a ubiquitous, connected, and continuously online world.

Chapter 4 discusses the evolution of recruitment. It emphasizes the impact of social recruiting on society and how it shapes a new reality in the brave new online world. In this chapter, we talk about the promises of a new El Dorado to jobseekers who create new jobs or seek for employment anywhere in the world. Finally, this chapter discusses the trend of gamification in recruitment.

Chapter 5 talks about you. It provides suggestions to set up your personal branding strategy. It explains why it is vital to start branding yourself early on and why you should Google yourself periodically. The chapter offers information on how to remove unwanted data from the

Internet. It also discusses many stories of people who either found or lost a job due to social media. Finally, the chapter concludes with a recap of what we should do to fortify our brand ecosystem.

Chapter 6 concludes with a forecast on personal branding and social recruiting. It discusses new trends in social recruiting and job searching. It explains the impact of Big Data predictions and People Analytics applications. The chapter highlights the effects of social media in the brave new online world and dares to ask its readers whether or not the book met its promises. Finally, the book's author provides his thoughts on a global discussion regarding a concept that is still evolving and growing.

CHAPTER 1

From Brands to Humans

This chapter at a glance:

- Why branding?
- The evolution of branding
- Emotional marketing
- The four passions of branding
- Passionate branding

PewDiePie

Real Name: Felix Arvid Ulf Kjellberg
Country: Sweden
Social Media: YouTube
His Story: If you like video games then chances are you've heard of PewDiePie, the leading video game commentator of all time! A former Industrial Economics student, Ulf Kjellberg began elaborating his videos back in 2010, and by 2012 he already had a fan base of 1 million subscribers. He dropped out of university and started working on a hot dog stand to fund his business. Luckily for him, he wouldn't need his degree to make a living. Felix's fan base kept growing at exponential levels. Today he has over 39 million subscribers, and his videos have been viewed over 10 billion times, making him the most subscribed YouTube Channel. He has a fortune of approximately 12 million dollars.

(James 2018)

Why Branding?

Before we start talking about social media, recruiting strategies, intelligence software applications, video resumes, personal recruiting strategies, and other new terms and concepts in business, we need to step back and talk about branding. Why branding? Branding is more than just a logo, few graphic elements, colors, and slogans. A brand is a company's soul and personality. Our name has the same qualities as a brand when we communicate it in public. Whether the brand is Nike or someone named John Smith, what matters is how we "sell" it.

The notion of branding goes back to ancient Greek and Roman times when tradespeople used symbols and signs as a means to communicate what products they had on offer (Roper and Fill 2012). The concept of branding might also have come from the earliest forms of organized farming, in which farmers would burn a mark into the skin of cattle to differentiate and establish their ownership over the animals (Roper and Fill 2012). What we can decipher from these arguments is that the concept of branding stems from two main ideas: (i) Brands are used to communicate a message through association for a target audience, and (ii) brands function as a differentiating factor.

Today, brands are commonly explained as being "a manufacturer's way of adding value and giving its products or services an individuality that sets it apart from the rest [i.e., the products and services of competitors]" (Roper and Fill 2012, p. 108). Moreover, the notion that brands add value to products and services that goes beyond their functional attributes seems to be widely acknowledged by marketing researchers and professionals today. However, whether these branding theories can be extended to include humans is still a topic of discussion among academics (Shepherd 2005).

A growing body of academic researchers have been investigating human behavior and personal branding in the online world (Chen 2013; Gandini 2016; Harris and Rae 2011; Khedher 2015; Labrecque, Markos, and Milne 2011; Lair, Sullivan, and Cheney 2005; Parmentier, Fischer, and Reuber 2013). For instance, when discussing celebrity brands, Roper and Fill (2012, p. 190) explain: "the image of the sports star no longer belongs to the club but the individual sportsperson in recognition of the fact that the individual has now also become a brand."

The concept that a person can be a brand name as well was first formally discussed by Kotler and Levy (1969). They write that "personal marketing is an endemic human activity, from the employee trying to impress his boss to the statesman trying to win the support of the public" [and] "thus, the 'product' can take many forms, and this is the first crucial point in the case for broadening the concept of marketing" (p. 12). The primitive notion of personal branding goes back in time as Kotler and Levy argue that there are similarities in trade practices between the modern times and the ancient times in relation to marketing goods, services, and humans.

Can a person be a "product" and, therefore, a brand? This dilemma could be both criticized and supported. From an ethical point of view, one would argue that humans should not function as products. From a practical point of view, it is in the very nature of humans to compete based on their skills and qualifications. Who is the strongest, fastest, or fittest? Who scores more goals or baskets? Who receives better grades in class? Who earns more money at work? Just as marketing teams aim to promote their products' competitive advantages, humans do the same in any aspect of their life.

There are many issues that we need to consider in this debate. Personal branding evangelists tend to emphasize the idea of "Work with what you've got! . . . And make it special" (Peters 1999, cited in Shepherd 2005, p. 593). On the contrary, critics argue that in marketing, products respond to the market's demand and adapt to customers' needs. Once a product is deemed as no longer adhering to this fundamental marketing principle, it becomes obsolete and is removed from the market. Can we claim the same for humans?

Humans always adapted to new living conditions. If today's fiercely competitive marketplace demands humans to stand out from the crowd and promote their expertise or uniqueness, personal branding seems to offer them an escape route. Shepherd (2005) highlights the many brand challenges that forced consumers to become more skeptical about marketing, such as brand conflicts, brand abundance, overpromising, or marketing scams. However, as Shepherd (2005) argues, we should not discard the possibility of extending and applying the marketing principles to people.

Marketing scholars contend that brands can have human characteristics since customers can more quickly generate feelings with other humans than they do with objects. Experts in marketing manage brands strategically to make the necessary associations between the product and its customers (Khedher 2015). For example, the new iPhone X had managed to generate so much anticipation and enthusiasm among its clientele that buyers chose to wait in long queues outside the Apple outlets, all night long, wanting to be the first to get hold of the new model (Gibbs 2017). What makes thousands of people anticipate the arrival of a product with such passion and loyalty?

Just like humans, a brand also has attributes such as skills, personality, and relationships (Biel 1997, cited in Fill 2005). Brand skills are the technical characteristics and functional abilities that the brand has and delivers. Brand personality refers to the brand's "fundamental traits concerning lifestyle and perceived values, such as being bland, adventurous, exciting, boring or caring" (Biel 1997, cited in Fill 2005, p. 394). Lastly, brand relationships refer to how each brand interacts with its consumers. Nowadays, we see brands chatting with customers on social media, providing health tips, career advice, safety instructions, and lifestyle tips.

It appears that there are several similarities and a healthy relationship when it comes to distinguishing between traditional and personal branding practices. Humans can be a brand, and the reverse is also true, in marketing parlance (Khedher 2015). The next section discusses the evolution of branding and how humans started adopting brand practices in the way they communicate.

The Evolution of Branding

For decades, brand building has been a mixed blessing for both companies and marketers. Branding is a mature concept that evolved over the past few years because of the rapid growth in the use of the Internet, particularly social media. Companies like Procter & Gamble have been the precursors of building strong brands by using mass media. The market today is highly competitive with new products, services, and brands that appear online. In such a turbulent marketplace, traditional brands try to protect their reputation and maintain their lead over competitors. Due to the barrage of mass media, individuals are overwhelmed with millions of messages or advertisements; this in turn leads to products losing their identity and becoming nearly invisible in the marketplace.

Marketing is changing and has reached the point where companies can no longer market directly to the masses. The traditional way of building a brand by using mass media is obsolete and has nothing to do with the emergence of new ways of doing it today. Traditional mass media is no longer communicating to consumers' subconscious. That is why brands investigate alternative ways to build stronger and more humane brands.

This complicated and lengthy process is both a science and an art. There are no good recipes to follow, but there are feelings to develop. With the rise of digital media, alternative approaches are coming out. This section aims to explain the evolution of the concept of branding mainly to identify the new, "prototype" approaches that pioneers in marketing are putting into practice today.

The purpose of branding is to permit companies to be identified and to differentiate their products or services from others. Brands aim for recognition and recall. The Saatchi & Saatchi CEO worldwide and chairman from 1997 until 2016, Kevin Roberts, says, "the race to brand led to commodification—the erosion of distinctions, rapid imitation of innovation, higher standards of product performance and—accelerated by technology—a final transfer of power to consumers" (Manafu 2004). Indeed, it helps the customer to choose when a purchase decision is involved. Identification, differentiation, and recognition are the keywords of strong brands. As branding is turning into a complicated business concept, successful brands aim strategically to stimulate customers' real feelings.

Why are people willing to pay more to buy Christian Dior? Are Christian Dior dresses more than a regular product? A brand is a set of associations and expectations for a company's products or services; in other words, it is an implicit promise of what the buyer can expect and what meaning it has in a customer's life. As a consequence, branding is not a combination of logos, slogan, or advertising. It is an ensemble of implicit messages that cultivate a deeper level of connection with the customer. Consequently, the established brand–customer relationship will influence humans to prefer and choose a specific group of products or services over others.

Brand loyalty is what marketers have been trying to achieve for years with mass advertising. They have created an exceptional connection with the masses via TV commercials, telling stories to garner mass attention. The traditional marketing model used mass media to reach a broad audience, which has been tested successfully and widely discussed among professionals. However, this model is considered old-fashioned and, therefore, no longer satisfactory, as it makes no emotional bonds with the target group.

There are several factors involved in the branding process that can explain the limited impact of the use of traditional mass media. The clients' needs and behaviors are constantly changing, which affects how they receive messages. For instance, a person who is tired will be less likely to listen to what brands have to say on television. The competitors' strategies will also influence the way marketers build their brands. A good example is the commercial battle between Apple and Samsung. If one of these two brands stop being aggressive over each other, they will probably have to implement another strategy that seems relevant to their perceived brand image.

It is certain that the process of branding is complicated and companies cannot merely rely on mass media and traditional advertising anymore for brand building. There are too many messages, and an individual cannot absorb them all. People try to avoid them every day and install "TiVo" in their house or subscribe to Netflix and other streaming services. Consumers watch thousands of messages every day in subways, streets, TV, newspapers, buses, taxis, stadiums, public parks, shopping malls, universities, e-mails, and websites.

If branding cannot rely on mass media anymore, what strategy should marketing professionals adopt? Nowadays, customers collect information from everywhere. They do not expect to learn about a new product or service from the mass media. A Facebook friend's recommendation of a product or a good review on booking.com is a more efficient way to reach more customers.

Multinational corporations like Nike, Starbucks, or Marks & Spencer had at one time to manage an identity crisis due to customer rebellion. The closing of plants, decline in the quality of work conditions, the disrespect shown to the environment, and unfair trade practices are issues raised commonly today. Moreover, it is a fact that customers do not understand the reason for the huge money spent on mass media and wonder why corporates should be spending all that money on mere advertisements when there are many other critical social concerns that need resolution, such as racism, discrimination, inequality in the society, and environmental pollution. So what can be an excellent strategy to communicate with modern consumers?

Emotional Branding

Branding is not only about ubiquity, visibility, and functions; it is about bonding emotionally with people in their daily life. Only when a product or a service kindles an emotional dialogue with the consumer, can this product or service qualify to be a brand. (Gobe 2010)

Emotional marketing has become a buzzword in business. As customers get more and more critical and suspicious, companies have to behave like humans. For years, companies have focused on profit, economies of scale, and mass media advertising to reach a broad audience, but along the way forgot to care about what keeps them in business—their customers. Emotional marketing treats customers as human beings and involves emotions and feelings in the brand–customer relationship. Nowadays, brands try to listen and discuss with consumers. For example, Procter & Gamble abandoned the "better, cleaner, sharper" advertising model of their line of products to go with the model of "proud sponsors of moms" that salutes all the mothers for all the sacrifices they made to see their kids succeed in life.

The president of Hallmark Loyalty, Scott Robinette, writes that "emotionally loyal customers relate to the brand as they might to other human beings—feelings of affection, a common history, possibly a sense of trust and two-way" (Robinette et al. 2000, p. 2). Creating emotional connections or sharing familiar stories is the new way of thinking. Companies now understand this process and focus on their brand identity, the living experience, and the emotional connection with people.

An interesting point of view comes from Kevin Roberts (2006) and his concept of Lovemarks. In his book *Lovemarks—The Future Beyond*

Brands he explains the simple evolution of brands to "Lovemarks"—from simple products to trademarks and then brands. Now that people adore products and become loyal to them, brands become Lovemarks that embrace emotions and talk straight to people's hearts. The iPhone, Samsung Galaxy, Starbucks, and The Body Shop are some examples of brands that turned into Lovemarks. Roberts makes a point that "Lovemarks are created and owned by the people who love them." With Lovemarks the process is entirely different than with brands. A stronger tie is created to replace the information of what a product can offer to consumers. Lovemarks create stories and experiences that their customers are willing to share on social media for free. Marketing is not a narrative anymore but a passionate love story.

The Four Passions of Branding Innovation

We have to do it differently. There are more possibilities, many choices, and we have to hit the audience quicker and in the heart. (Roberts 2006, p. 12)

Branding innovation today can be summed up by four types of passion:

- **P**assion for Values
- **P**assion for Ideas
- **P**assion for Life
- **P**assion for People

Passion for Values

Mass advertising can help build brands, but authenticity is what makes them last. If people believe they share values with a company, they will stay loyal to a brand. (Schultz and Yang 1999, p. 23)

Companies tend to forget their values or at least how to publicly communicate them. However, identifying values and building a corporate culture is now a primordial asset. For customers, a great company is a company that cares! As a consequence, to create an emotional connection and healthy relationship, customers and employees have to identify themselves with the corporate values.

Companies need to have a clear identity and so have identifiable values. Those values help each group to differentiate and establish a credible, reliable, and trustworthy long-term relationship with its customers. Modern consumers seek respect, passion, honesty, responsibility, and creativity. Today's message is: "Be respectful, passionate, responsible, and innovative, and I will give you my trust and my loyalty." In 2018, Nike decided to feature Colin Kaepernick, the San Francisco 49ers quarterback, in the thirtieth-anniversary "Just Do It" campaign. Colin Kaepernick has been banned from NFL due to his decision to kneel during the national anthem at the start of an American football game, as a form of protest against injustice and police brutality in America. This decision resulted in a storm of discussions in America, with consumers either praising Nike for standing by Kaepernick or burning their Nike shoes in public.

Brands like The Body Shop have a clear identity and positioning. It is easy for the customer to create a connection with that brand and be able to identify themselves with it. Anita Roddick, Founder of The Body Shop, had a clear understanding of what values could generate. From one outlet in Brighton, UK, in 1976, she established a global brand with 1900 stores in almost 50 countries. Roddick's philosophy of living in a better world is reflected by the values of her company and products. The Body Shop highly promotes corporate social responsibility and environmental protection policies. The brand is supporting community trade, refusing to practice animal testing, activating self-esteem, defending human rights, and protecting the planet. All these values are creating the "aura" of The Body Shop brand.

Passion for Ideas

Seth Godin (2009), author of *Purple Cow: Transform Your Business by Being Remarkable*, argues the more choices we have, the more confused we, the customers, become. As there is such abundance of product offerings in the market, the customer journey becomes an odyssey. Should they go online or visit a brick-and-mortar store? Should they wait until the new product hits the market or should they buy it immediately?

Awareness is not a priority anymore, but big ideas and concepts are. Seth Godin uses the term "Purple Cow" as a metaphor for a "Remarkable" product. It is the passion for ideas. People have to be fascinated by innovative products and services. Companies have to reinvest in building something new and outstanding to be notable on the market. In this case, the remarkable product will have to be targeted at a specific niche market and not directed at masses to be successful.

Kevin Roberts (2006) argues never to give customers what they want but to give them what they never dreamed possible. Word of Mouth marketing results to five times more sales than a paid media impression. Also, studies have shown that consumers are 90 percent more likely to select a brand recommended by a friend (Erskine 2016). Godin calls it "the idea virus." If the product is noteworthy, a viral communication will take place by itself. Customers will not only buy the product, they will also share it on social media. They will make selfies and brag about it. There are millions of YouTube videos showing users unboxing the new iPhone or a new toy. People love success stories, and they are thrilled when they become part of them.

Good ideas can come from anyone. The new mobile application stores (mainly App Store and Google Play Store) provide the platform where ideas flourish. Entrepreneurs, web developers, and ordinary businesspeople are all engaged in finding the new design that people will love. Already there are many examples of such applications that received global acceptance, such as WhatsApp, Viber, Uber, Instagram, Angry Birds, Spotify, and Google Maps.

Passion for Life

There is nothing to it. You only have to hit the right note at the right time, and the instrument plays itself. (Johann Sebastian Bach, as quoted by Erskine (2005, p. 75))

A new marketing approach is to let customers and employees "live the brand." Social media allowed people to talk freely about their experiences with products. Nowadays, customers have countless options such as blog posts, customer reviews, thumbs-up and thumbs-down, the "like" button, and emoji to show their support or rejection of brands.

Brands sponsor and produce live events, games, and competitions to strengthen the emotional connections with their audiences. These "living media" allowed brands to be more innovative and remarkable in their interactions with the audience. Red Bull is a pioneering brand in such marketing approaches that satisfy the "wings" brand concept. Red Bull either produces or sponsors remarkable events in various fields, such as in arts and music, with the Red Bull Flying Bach, the High Culture meets Urban Art, the Red Bull Music Festivals, and so on. Also, Red Bull is highly active in sports by organizing and supporting events such as the B-Boys show (motorbikes), the Formula 1 Abu Dhabi Grand Prix, the Red Bull Storm Chase (windsurf), the Dakar Rally, and hundreds of sponsored activities all over the world.

Advertising was essential, but now the integration of media, communication, and marketing is vital. The increasing media costs left space for alternative media vehicles that entertain, nurture, educate, and sensitize customers. At its best, public relations is a strategic marketing and branding tool to accomplish a stated business objective.

Passion for People

Employees want to love the company they work for, and if they do—big surprise—they do better work. All of a sudden, the brand is about more than just marketing. Passion for people is the last point and maybe the most important one. Branding is not only about external communication. Indeed, internal branding is essential and functions as an asset to building a brand image. Branding is the soul of the company, and the employees are the first to live the brand. It is more than necessary to align the corporate culture with the brand's values. Internal communications and branding today create strong bonds between the company and its people.

Nowadays, employees are the brand's real "ambassadors." They are the face and personality of each brand. After all, the employees are standing on the frontline when facing the customers. Successful brands have quickly realized that the first customers of each product are its employees. The happier the employees are, the best the brand will be communicated and served.

Employees are the ones who can emotionally connect with customers. Nevertheless, companies often overlook their most critical audience— their employees. Employees are without doubt an asset that companies have to involve in the branding process. Engaging employees will convert them into advocates for the brand identity.

How can companies motivate employees to support the brand? In a *Harvard Business Review* online article titled "Selling the Brand Inside," Mitchell (2002) argues on the necessity to inform employees about the brand's goals and actions. He writes,

> Why is internal marketing so important? First, because it is the best way to help employees make a powerful emotional connection to the products and services you sell. Without that connection, employees are likely to undermine the expectations set by your advertising.

Employees do not always understand what the company promises to the public. Human resource departments plan initiatives such as intranet discussions, internal competitions, social invitations, newsletters, and digital signage, among others. Such internal communication initiatives aim to strengthen the values, mission, general strategy, and the vision of the brand to employees.

Employees have to be brand ambassadors from the bottom-up to top-down. The entire organization has to engage in internal branding efforts to support the frontline employees. If there is no coordination and alignment between what the brand entails and how the employees behave, the audience will receive mixed messages. Such a lack of clear communication will lead to failures in branding and marketing.

For a study at Arizona State University on "brand confluence," researchers hired actors to interact with customers pretending to be sales-people (Conner 2014). Some of the actors were instructed to behave in a way that was highly aligned with the attributes of the brand they were selling, and some others did the opposite, by acting misaligned. The study showed that the customers who interacted with the highly aligned em-ployees with the brand's attributes rated the brand as desirable, trustwor-thy, and valuable. On the contrary, customers did not seem to make a clear distinction between the brand and its disengaged employees. Therefore, the customers commented negatively on the brand overall, only because of a bad experience at the point of sale.

Because employees are directly in contact with the customers, they have a lot of influence on the brand image. That is why a strategic plan has to be implemented by companies to build a robust internal communication that would positively affect their public perception. Employees have to know and represent the brand values. Also, employees have to understand and feel part of the strategy that drives the general business. In other words, the primary objective of internal communication experts is to motivate employees to live the brand.

How can companies achieve it? Primarily, storytelling helps the company spread the message faster and easier. Second, simulating involves the training of people so that they can practice and boost their confidence before contacting customers. Third, selecting engages attentive recruitment from the HR division. The company must attract the best talents and the ones that are sharing universal values. Finally, surveying is saving money on the external communication, to study employee behaviors and receive constructive feedback.

In other words, active internal communication involves recruiting, interviewing, selecting, training, and increasing employees' career prospects. Rewarding and recognizing good work and leadership will help people to enhance motivation and to develop their sense of teamwork. If all these conditions apply, employees are living the brand, and ideally, they become the brand.

The key to managing the employee dimension of each brand is the ability to deliver to employees the following principles. Employees need a challenging job, a cause to believe in, a continuous learning environment, a fascinating career plan, personal involvement of the work tasks, a sense of ownership and accountability in the business, and positive recognition of excellence. In this way, employees will develop the internal drive and motivation to work for a company that cares about them. As a consequence, they will care about the customers and will treat them with respect.

Starbucks is a brand that quickly invested in the human factor and implemented the model that shows that great people, excellent work environment, and satisfied clients make good money and happy share-holders. Starbucks CEO, Howard Schulz, keeps repeating the brand's model in interviews and presentations. Schultz considers his company's employees as "brand ambassadors." The company uses the term "part-ners" to highlight their importance in delivering the Starbucks brand values. As the Starbucks CEO highlights, the brand was built "first on people, not on consumers; this is the opposite approach from that of the crackers-and-cereal companies" (Argenti 2007, p. 90). The Starbucks CEO recognizes that the most expensive advertising campaign will never erase the mistake of one coffee barista. Starbucks is an excellent example of a brand that managed to build a reputation from the heart and the strength of human spirit.

Passionate Branding

Branding has now a lot more choices to reach customers in various exciting ways with the four passions of branding innovation, as discussed in this chapter. Branding innovation needs to have a passion for values, ideas, life, and people. Passionate CEOs need passionate managers who will coach passionate employees. Today's marketing landscape requires creative ideas, feelings, exciting moments, and people who are willing to share the story and become the brand.

Consumers want to be a part of their favorite brand's story. They get emotionally attached to products and services. It looks like the time of the small and local grocery shop in the corner is gone. Nevertheless, custom-ers want to bring back that kind of relationship. It is a love story. They want to love and be loved. Through a variety of success stories in global branding, the first chapter set the scene for the rest. Branding is every-where, and that includes humans too. The next chapter builds a bridge between brands and humans to strengthen the book's argument that per-sonal branding is a serious business.

CHAPTER 2

Personal Branding

This chapter at a glance:

- Why are personal brands important?
- Definition of terms
- The evolution of personal branding
- Online social entertainment
- How to develop and maintain your brand?
- What makes a personal brand successful?

The Blonde Salad

Real Name: Chiara Ferragni
Country: Italy
Social Media: Blog and Instagram
Her Story: Chiara Ferragni, a 28-year-old Law student at Bocconi University in Milan, is one of the most successful bloggers to transition from amateur to professional. Starting The Blonde Salad in 2009, a fashion blog where she broadcasts her interests in fashion, photography, travel, and lifestyle, Ferragni quickly became a success online and currently receives over 110,000 daily hits on her site. However, that was only the beginning. Her blog generates only 30 percent of her revenue. Ferragni started forming partnerships with fashion brands and is expected to earn a total of 8 million dollars this year. She now has her shoe brand which has become unbelievably fortunate.

(James 2018)

Why Is Personal Branding Important?

To begin our investigation into the development of personal branding in business, we need to first examine specific key and relevant theoretical constructs. This chapter provides an understanding of how branding theories can be extended to include humans. Moreover, this chapter explains how social media has had an immediate impact on the development of personal branding.

Personal branding has evolved as an essential strategy for working individuals. The proliferation of social networking websites such as Facebook and YouTube allowed online users to develop stronger brands to display their skills and passions. Greer (2010) writes that "in a business world that's increasingly dominated by social media, mastering the ability to sell [oneself] in cyberspace has become one of the most important skills a worker can possess" (p. 30). In simple words, an online personal brand is someone's resume with unique personality characteristics.

Personal branding can offer a vital competitive advantage in today's job market. The competition for finding a good job is fiercer than ever before, and the chances to stand out from the crowd are limited. Too many candidates hold university degrees and other kinds of credentials. Formal education does not seem to offer the competitive advantage as it used to in the past.

Nowadays, companies look for talents and natural-born leaders who will move the business forward. The pool of candidates is not limited to geographic locations. Any candidate from anywhere in the world can look for available jobs and apply online. Academic scholars investigate the best practices of personal branding to explain the means and methods people use to advance on their career (Gandini 2016; Gehl 2011; Harris and Rae 2011; Khedher 2015; Lair, Sullivan, and Cheney 2005; Rampersad 2008; Schawbel 2011). In today's globalized business environment the need to differentiate ourselves demonstrates personal leadership skills.

One's online image and reputation can be a differentiating factor among other job candidates (Gandini 2016). People are aiming for personal and professional success, and the notion that "if you do not brand yourself, others will" (Kaputa 2006, cited in Shepherd 2005, p. 590) appears to be an inconvenient truth. It seems that if you do not have an online account, recruiters get suspicious that you are hiding something. Personal branding is not only a YouTube channel or a LinkedIn account. It is everything that can be found online and relates to your name.

Social media is a powerful tool for personal branding. Users are willing to upload too much personal information online. The intention primarily is to communicate with their friends and to keep up with what's going on in their social circles. Nevertheless, any news, images, and comments they share online become their digital footprint that anyone can see. If a recruiter was to search for a potential candidate, any available information could be used either for or against the candidate.

Personal branding is not a fad, and we should not neglect it. The knowledge of how brands are created could be used toward someone's professional success. People should know the strengths, weaknesses, opportunities, and threats to their brand name. We try to impress a recruiter during a job interview by expressing the best of ourselves. So, why aren't we doing the same when we share information about ourselves online?

In broad terms, personal branding is how the audience perceives us. Which search keywords lead to our name? In what follows, we quote several brand-related terms to further our knowledge of personal branding.

Definition of Terms

Brand: An emotional association with the image or name of a particular company, product, or person.

Brand image: How the marketplace perceives the product/service.

Brand identity: The marketing strategy to achieve a unique brand image.

Brand positioning: How marketers position the brand by the market competitors.

Brand personality: A set of human characteristics that are attributed to a brand name such as sincerity, excitement, competence, sophistication, and ruggedness. Consumers see and treat the brand as a human being.

Personal branding: The effort of individuals and entrepreneurs to "differentiate themselves and stand out from a crowd by identifying and articulating their unique value proposition, whether professional or personal and then leverage it across platforms with a consistent message and image to achieve a specific goal" (Schawbel 2010, p. 6).

Self-presentation: A personal effort to communicate information to other people by displaying our skills and qualities (Labrecque, Markos, and Milne 2011).

Self-promotion: "Promoting one's self, events, accomplishments, victories, defeats, problems, and lessons learned to increase one's visibility to and awareness by others" (Deckers and Lacy 2012, p. 5).

The Evolution of Personal Branding

Personal branding is about expressing your authentic self by allowing you to be the person you are meant to be. The process of personal branding will help connect with your unique promise of value and employ it in the world. Your brand acts as a filter to help you make decisions that are congruent with who you are and what you stand for. It identifies what makes you unique and communicates your individuality to the people who need to know about you. (Chritton 2013)

Personal branding is about telling your unique story through words, visuals, tweets, and shares. It promises that people have equal opportunities to market themselves through the Internet and social media. Marketing strategies and theories that have been employed to brand products and services can now be extended to brand humans. This is not a new concept though. Kotler and Levy (1969) discussed how marketing efforts could be applied not only to products but also to services, persons, and ideas. Today, the notion of humans being a brand is recognized among researchers because humans "1) can be strategically managed and 2) have additional associations and features of a brand" (Khedher 2015, p. 19).

The idea that humans can brand themselves became popular in the late 1990s. Initially, several authors started publishing self-help books (Shepherd 2005). These books wanted to boost their readers' confidence to communicate and express their views publicly. Peters (1997) was the first to mention the term *personal branding* as a sign of distinction among people. He claimed that as a result of the industrial revolution, people started to look alike, having the same level of education and professional skills. Therefore, as Peters (1997) argued in an article titled "The Brand Called You," we are living in the era of personal revolution that all people could be their brand and CEOs of "Me, Inc."

However, the mass adoption of social media developed a new mindset in personal branding. Nowadays, social media users take advantage of the unlimited possibilities that social networking websites offer to express their views, skills, and qualities publicly. In other words, social media developed an online environment where personal branding is not an exclusive privilege for a select few, such as famous CEOs and celebrities and their luxurious lifestyles. Instead, personal branding promises that every person deserves to be heard by others, so they can decide whether to support the individual or not.

Today, online users share their passions on social media. They publish content and personalize their digital profiles to connect with people who have the same hobbies and interests. In the past, the need was to connect with classmates, colleagues, and generally people we knew. Now, the trend is to share content with anyone in the world who likes what we like.

Is social media the only technology that ever promoted personal branding? Of course not. Traditional mass media such as newspapers, magazines, radio, and television cultivated the notion of personal branding as well. The mass media world includes journalists, actors, singers, and other types of celebrities who used the traditional channels of communication to become famous. Nevertheless, social media simplified the development process and thus expanded the notion of personal branding. With social media, humans of all age groups and nationalities can promote themselves and their ideas.

Online users aim through personal branding to communicate their uniqueness and increase their popularity. Although there is no secret recipe to build a successful brand, such efforts require a well-implemented plan and a great deal of luck. Arruda (2009) argues that users need to follow the three-stage process—"extract, express, and exude"—to develop a unique and attractive brand to a mass audience. The three-stage process involves (i) identifying one's unique value proposition, (ii) expressing views and opinions that either trigger curiosity or provide original information, and (iii) using the best technical means to display the message.

First, we need to find out what makes us unique. What is the one thing that our audience would benefit from following us on Instagram or YouTube? As soon as we identify our value proposition, the next step is to work on how best to express our views. We should master our communication skills to express our thoughts openly. Finally, we should choose the channel that best suits our needs. For example, successful personal branding stories could be found on YouTube, Facebook, Instagram, Vine, or regular blogs. There is no one-size-fits-all solution in successful personal branding.

Arruda (2009) also argues that personal brands need to express their messages with *clarity*, *consistency*, and *constancy*. Clarity is an essential quality of personal branding because

> it is critical to be clear and authentic about who you are, and what you are not. You must understand your unique promise of value, and how this promise enables you to influence people who can help you achieve your goals. (p. 409)

Our brand should be consistent and easily recognizable by the audience. Just like the legendary music band Rolling Stones that has a unique, transparent, and consistent sound, humans should maintain a steady and constant relationship with the target audience.

What about constancy? Arruda (2009) mentions Oprah Winfrey as an example of a successful celebrity who turned out to become a widely recognized brand name. He writes that

> one of the most successful, visible, and constant personal brands, both commercially and personally, is Oprah Winfrey. With her weekly television show, book club, magazine, numerous media appearances, and casual appearances in grocery stores and restaurants, Oprah is consistently visible and has maintained an incredibly strong brand over a very long career. (p. 410)

We are just like brands. We want our friends, followers, and connections to find and like our content whenever and wherever we post it.

We become social entertainers, and social media is our stage. We feel that our posts have an impact on people. We want to please and engage them more in our interests. For example, online users who play video games want to share their passion with other gamers. Other users decide to unbox the new iPhone or to review a new gadget. Social media users have to prove they are genuine and worthy of following consistently. They ask for approval from likes, views, and thumbs-up signs. Welcome to the era of online social entertainment.

Online Social Entertainment

Viral videos such as the ALS Ice Bucket Challenge, the Harlem Shake, the #HuhChallenge, the Mannequin Challenge, the Kiki challenge, the Hot Pepper Challenge, #SoGoneChallenge, the Sausage Rap, and the Cinnamon Challenge have something in common. They all became online trends involving millions of people who uploaded their videos to YouTube. Due to these and many other similar patterns, people started dumping a bucket of ice over their head, dancing next to moving cars, standing still, dancing with funny costumes, or tasting unusual foods. Overall, these trends entertained people on social media. Nevertheless, the term *online social entertainment* means much more than that.

Online social entertainment includes "playing collaborative online games, reading email, chatting online (e.g., MSN), maintaining a personal website or blog, and joining discussion forums or virtual communities (e.g., MySpace or Facebook) on social networking sites (SNS)" (Lee and Wu 2013, p. 169). People use technological features such as live video streaming, instant messengers, online gaming platforms, music streaming services, and social networking websites to have fun and increase their popularity.

Today's online environment requires more interaction with the online community and consistent content sharing. While social networking websites aim to build and maintain relationships among the online users, social entertainment defines people's effort to create and share content that will please the online community and generate more views and likes (Panigrahi 2018). In other words, social media provides a whole new environment where users get entertained and entertain others by posting content online.

There are many online social entertainment services. The most famous social networking website that offers entertainment services is YouTube. The following are some interesting facts and numbers about the number one video streaming platform, and the second most popular search engine in the world after Google.

YouTube Statistics—2018

- YouTube was launched on February 14, 2005 by Steve Chen, Chad Hurley, and Jawed Karim. Now it is the second most visited website in the world after Google.
- The very first YouTube video was uploaded on April 23, 2005.
- The total number of people who use YouTube is 1,300,000,000.
- As much as 300 hours of video are uploaded to YouTube every minute!
- Almost 5 billion videos are watched on YouTube every single day.
- YouTube gets over 30 million visitors per day.
- In an average month, eight out of ten 18- to 49-year-olds watch YouTube.
- By 2025, half of the viewers under age 32 will not subscribe to a pay-TV service.
- Six out of 10 people prefer online video platforms to live TV.
- The total number of hours of video watched on YouTube each month is 3.25 billion.
- As many as 10,113 YouTube videos generated over 1 billion views.
- As much as 80 percent of YouTube views are from outside of the United States.
- The average number of mobile YouTube video views per day is 1,000,000,000.
- The average mobile viewing session lasts more than 40 minutes. This is up by more than 50 percent, year over year.
- Female users are 38 percent and male users are 62 percent.
- User percentage by age: 18 to 24 years—11 percent, 25 to 34 years—23 percent, 35 to 44 years—26 percent, 45 to 54 years—16 percent, 50 to 64 years—8 percent, 65+ years—3 percent, unknown age—14 percent.

- More than half of YouTube views come from mobile devices.
- YouTube's mobile revenue is up to two times year over year.
- YouTube overall, and even YouTube on mobile alone, reaches more 18- to 34-year-olds and 18- to 49-year-olds than any cable network in the United States.
- The number of hours people spend watching videos on You-Tube is up by 60 percent year over year, the fastest growth we have seen in two years.
- You can navigate YouTube in a total of 76 different languages (covering 95 percent of the Internet population).
- YouTube has launched local versions in more than 88 countries.
- As much as 9 percent of U.S. small businesses use YouTube.
- Approximately 20 percent of the people who start your video will leave after the first 10 seconds.

(YouTube 2018)

YouTube is not the only social entertainment platform though. Other social networking websites and mobile applications offer features for community users to post content for entertainment purposes as well. The most popular social networking websites such as Facebook, Twitter, Pinterest, and Instagram added features to increase user spontaneity to post live videos and stories and to create trends in music, photography, video gaming, and television. Mobile applications, such as UStream and Livestream, allow users to record anything from their phones and stream it online. Nowadays, we notice that even the most advanced television networks use content from live stream services.

With the use of technology, everyone can be famous. We see online TV series made only for YouTube TV. We know singers who become famous after successfully covering a favorite song and video gamers who post walkthrough videos. We see rising star athletes who display their skills so that recruiters and talent scouts will notice them. Is it always about talent? Not at all. People post their fail videos displaying their silly or severe accidents or share their pranks with their friends to get more subscribers to their YouTube channels. The list of success stories in personal branding is endless.

Online entertainment is a social phenomenon. The industry experiences a rapid growth by replacing traditional media and entertainment services. The mass adoption of online streaming services such as Netflix and Spotify, as well as the illegal torrent websites that allow unlawful downloading of movies and music albums, resulted in the shutdown of video clubs and music record shops. Since March 2017, YouTube launched their new streaming service YouTube TV, which is a cable-free TV streaming service that collaborates with major broadcast and favorite cable networks.

The new social entertainment landscape provides opportunities for people to promote their skills and interests through their media channels. Personal branding is a new form of communication that people use to get in touch with others while aiming to stand out from the crowd and increase their popularity. The modern workplace includes new job titles such as influencers, content developers, social media curators, community organizers, Snapchatters, YouTubers, viners, vloggers, trend spotters, reviewers, and social media evangelists. The workplace of the future promises even more niche jobs that we have not heard so far. So think again. Does personal branding matter? Here is what you should know to develop your brand.

Develop and Maintain Your Brand

The modern labor market is more demanding and competitive than ever. The positions available in the job market are very limited in number, which makes the need to differentiate even stronger. Today's jobseekers aim at having a distinct personal brand to offer them with more opportunities for work anywhere in the world. Horton (2011) argues that the development of our brand ensures that we have an active role in the job selection process and are ready to develop our career as professionals.

Modern organizations take the opportunity to use the social networking websites to search for talents. Personal branding turns to be an essential part of the hiring process. Labrecque, Markos, and Milne (2011) write about the importance of online tools in everyday marking since "everyone has the power to be their own brand and a person's main job is to be his or her own marketer." The concept that everyone can brand themselves is a game changer in job seeking. People can now brand themselves according to their desires and build their fan base, before even finishing high school.

Social media has become an online database of all sorts of resumes. People set up their online profiles to share their passions and interests. Employers admit that they check online to hire talented people, especially in fields such as sales, advertising, entertainment, and design. Sometimes, spotting a rare talent can happen accidentally while a recruiter is spending some time online. Hiring is now a process that can take place anytime and anywhere.

The story of the famous 19-year-old DJ Alan Walker is a good example of spontaneous talent spotting and career building. Based on Walker's video biography on YouTube titled "Unmasked (Episode 1)," it was 2012 when the Norwegian amateur video gamer Alan Walker got fascinated while watching a YouTube video on how to create music using nothing else but his computer. Having a basic background in music theory, Alan Walker watched online video tutorials to learn how to play electronic dance music (EDM). Two years later he released his first EDM piece "Fade" via the record label NoCopyrightSounds. The piece quickly became a top hit among the EDM fans and attracted the attention of Gunnar Greve, who became Walker's manager. Now, Alan Walker's transformation from a 19-year-old from Bergen, Norway, who was writing music in his bedroom, to be one of the most popular DJs in the world can be considered a stellar example of personal branding.

It is no secret that employers and recruiters look to people's social media accounts to get more information about a potential candidate. Social screening is a stage in the hiring process that provides recruiters with the information required for evaluating someone's character and the possibilities to fit into the organizational culture. Many HR managers admit that they negatively assess a candidate when they check his/her Facebook or Instagram profile to find inappropriate images, too many selfies, impolite statements, and misuse of language (Papakonstantinidis 2014).

What can you do to develop your brand? First of all, you need to know who you are and be ready to share what you love. Ask yourself: What is the one thing I am very good at and I love doing? Will people also like it? Personal branding begins by establishing a clear identity that the person will be able to communicate to a specific audience (Labrecque, Markos, and

Milne 2011). Personal branding should express the real you or to some extent a refined version of you. If you fake who you are, sooner or later people will know. Your content should be unique or at least a better version of what is already out there. The online world is full of opportunities as long as you can offer a strong value proposition to your target audience. Otherwise, the online community will not remember you.

One would say that having a university degree is enough to start a career. Yes, that is true, but having a degree does not make your online brand successful. Recruiters do not focus on your skills; rather, they focus on your value. You could grab recruiters' attention if you can increase your value and credibility through your refined communication skills and carefully maintained social media profiles. Demonstrate your abilities and invite people to love your passions. Show them what kind of personality and attributes you are bringing to the organization. Tell them your story, and if recruiters hire you, then you will know that you both have a perfect match.

What about maintaining a personal brand? This stage is probably harder to achieve. People get easily bored, and they are in pursuit of something new that will please them. Personal brands need to focus on clarity, consistency, and constancy (Arruda 2009). Individuals select specific social networking websites such as Facebook, Instagram, YouTube, Vine, Twitter, Wordpress, and LinkedIn to communicate their brand. Morton (2012) writes, "clarity and consistency are essential to creating an effective brand." Consistency across all social media platforms is crucial to maintaining your audience.

Any marketing strategy starts by analyzing the product and identifying the target audience. Similarly, a personal branding strategy should emphasize on establishing a fan base (target audience) and offering a unique and creative service. Original and creative content provides the best solution to attract your audience, whereas being relevant is about how to get your fan base to keep coming back for more information (Allen 2011). When you display your skills and expertise, you need to make sure you know more than your average fan. For example, many users post reviews from new gadgets such as phones, tablets, and wearable items. Usually, these online reviewers either aim to be the first to post about a new product or they offer valuable information to their viewers. If they do not do it well, someone else will.

What Makes a Personal Brand Successful?

We are citizens of a highly digitalized society where we value almost everything according to its popularity index. The most valuable asset that differentiates us from others is our personality. In the world of social media, the second most valuable asset seems to be our reputation. Regardless of our age and gender, whether we are a 15-year-old high school student who plays video games or an 80-year-old grandma who maintains a blog with cooking recipes, our online persona provides us with countless business opportunities.

The question remains, then, what should we do to stand out in a today's competitive marketplace? Matthew Jones (2017) interviewed the famous tech entrepreneur Manu Goswami, who is known online with the nickname Swish, to share his thoughts on the advantages of developing and maintaining a strong personal brand. Swish is a 20-year-old university student from Toronto. His online profile mentions that he is a UN Youth Ambassador, campus editor for LinkedIn, and TEDx speaker. Some of his most outstanding achievements are winning the Startup Canada's Young Entrepreneur competition and gaining the highest recognition as UN's Outstanding Youth Leader.

The following are some of Swish's responses regarding the importance of personal branding. First, he argues that a brand establishes credibility. "A huge way to combat that perceived lack of experience is to position yourself as a thought leader." Second, a personal brand creates a secure professional network. "When you interview someone, you can build a good connection with them that you can leverage later on—someone that you can then talk to and get help from." Third, a personal brand offers job security.

> There's almost no job in the changing world we live in that's safe. If you're doing something that you're passionate about, you're going to find both personal and professional hurdles along the way. The best thing you can do to provide job security is to have a personal brand that you can always fall back on.

The 20-year-old tech entrepreneur underlines that there is no guaranteed success with personal branding but "all you're doing is simply increasing the likelihood of a successful outcome." If people want to start building a personal brand Swish suggests that primarily people should "realize that a lot of the tools that young people are on currently can be turned into a way to build a personal brand." Social networking websites and mobile applications provide us with opportunities to produce unique content and share it online. He states that

> influencing the way people see you on that platform as an online avatar or persona and changing that to focus on a particular subject can just be the simple fix that you have to make for you to make others realize your value.

Another interesting tip that Swish provides in his interview is, "to start reaching out to people that are already building strong personal brands within your field of interest and asking to interview or meet with them." Also, as we mentioned earlier in this chapter, finding the right medium is crucial. Swish responds,

> the last thing you can do to get started is to find your medium and go all in. Look at audio, visual, or written content—figure out what you are the best at—and find platforms that allow you to showcase that and become the best at it.

Personal branding allows young entrepreneurs to add value to their services. Social media exposure could be fascinating and intimidating at the same time. People have to overcome their fear of getting out there and facing both praise and criticism. Swish's advice is to be real and accept who you are. "I think everyone has an interesting silver lining that he or she can find if he or she thinks about their life and what he or she is doing."

Personal branding is also appreciating and giving back to the community. Swish responds, "building a personal brand is not done in a vacuum—it is done with people. It is done with networking with people, helping people, and connecting people to one another." Finally, in his interview with Matthew Jones (2017), he concludes, the biggest thing you can do when building a personal brand is to not think about building yourself up as much as thinking about building other people up, which is what I believe is the basis to every strong personal brand.

The next chapter is about the generation that Swish and many young entrepreneurs belong to. This is a generation of users who were born and raised in technology and social media. To them, their neighborhood is the whole world that offers countless opportunities for business and pleasure.

CHAPTER 3

The Social Natives

This chapter at a glance:
- The hashtag generation
- From the digital natives to the social natives
- Recruiting the social natives
- Social nativity and the limitless opportunities

Jessi Smiles

Real Name: Jessica Vazquez
Country: United States
Social Media: Vines
Her Story: Jessi Smiles has more than 3.5 million followers. She is ranked on the list of top 30 Vine personalities in the world and is also the third most popular girl across all of the social media sites that she uses. Her Vines show her comedic side and general quirkiness that has been an absolute hit online, launching her into Vine stardom. According to BBC, Viners can charge advertisers somewhere in the ballpark of $1,000 per 100,000 followers for a video. Through advertising alone, Vazquez would have a reasonably comfortable income from each video she uploads merely by sitting on or growing that fan base of 3.5 million followers. Can you imagine? Making close to 35,000 dollars for a six-second video!

(James 2018)

The Hashtag Generation

Hashtags are words or phrases preceded by the pound sign (#) that function as keywords to allow social media users to engage in online discussions. Think of hashtags as "categories" of online threads that social media users follow to communicate with people they do not necessarily know. All they need to do is to follow or sometimes create the relevant hashtag and join a global discussion that the hashtag word or phrase signifies. For example, if you want to know what Twitter users talk about the Black Friday, you can search online to find the relevant hashtag #blackfriday and read what people write about last-minute deals or happenings.

How did it all start? The birth of the hashtag generation began from Twitter and has gone viral to all social networking sites. In 2007, the web developer Chris Messina suggested, in a tweet, that users should be grouping their topics using a keyword followed by the pound sign (#) to allow other users to follow particular conversations even if they were not connected. Although Twitter did not seem to favor Messina's idea, in October 2007, San Diego citizens started sharing information about the forest fires in the area. Messina suggested them to use the hashtag #SanDiegoFire every time they were tweeting news about the forest fires. That was it. The hashtag #SanDiegoFire became the first trend on Twitter as people managed to coordinate their efforts and to let everyone know about the critical situation. Since then, social media users include hashtags in a variety of topics and discussions, from critical sociopolitical events (#PrayForParis or #MeToo) to fun topics (#love or #instafood).

The hashtag is not the only way young people use to communicate. The early adopters of social media also communicate through posts, shares, likes, tweets, thumbs-up and thumbs-down, images, short videos, Vines, and many other ways that might be introduced by the time this book is published. The hashtag generation sees education differently. Young people learn best when training is given more entertainingly and randomly. Prensky (2001) argues that the new generation prefers reading websites and hyperlinks than pages and books. They have a sense of anxiety and impatience to understand many different and somehow interconnected topics. Young people prefer hands-on projects, multitasking learning by watching videos, completing online tasks, and applying theory to their everyday life.

The digital natives, whether in education or at work, are shaping the new social reality. They are members of the hashtag generation as they tend to form new social groups based on their similar interests and not based on whether they were classmates, neighbors, or family friends. For the hashtag generation, what matters is your impact and influence on social media, regardless of who you are. Many members of the hashtag generation are entering the business world, and it is worth keeping an eye on them.

This chapter furthers our understanding of the new generation of digital natives and social media enthusiasts who are entering the business world in a unique style. These young people are college graduates and, at the same time, famous YouTubers, online personas, style bloggers, community influencers, and niche celebrities with million followers. They adore social media and especially Facebook, Twitter, Instagram, and Snapchat. They love sharing pictures of themselves and their interests with their followers. Some of them want to become professional YouTubers by posting cover music videos, prank videos, car accidents on dashboard cameras (dashcams), or even videos of their unintentional accidents (fail videos). Everything for a thumbs-up!

How do digital natives think? Why do they want so eagerly to become famous? What will they gain? What do they prefer when it comes to social media use and job searching? Don't you agree that it is useful to learn more about them? The next section explains who digital natives are.

From the Digital Natives to Social Natives

It was in 2011 when the young advertiser Alec Brownstein introduced us to the Google Job Experiment. Back then, no one had an idea that this experiment would signify the beginning of a new era in job searching. Brownstein used Google AdWords to buy five keywords for only $6. He purchased the names of five famous creative advertising directors and used them as keywords in his campaign. Brownstein correctly assumed that at some point these people would type their names on Google, as many of us usually do. Once any of the five creative directors was googling his name, the following message appeared as paid advertisement "Googling yourself is a lot of fun. Hiring me is fun, too." The advertisement's link directed visitors to Brownstein's website, which allowed him to demonstrate his talent in copywriting. He got four interview calls, two job offers, and now Brownstein is working for one of the biggest advertising firms in New York.

Alec Brownstein's job searching experiment is one of those stories of young people who thought out of the box and used the new technologies as *digital natives* do. The term "digital natives" was first introduced by Prensky (2001) when he observed the new generation of freshmen college students. Prensky described them as a new generation of students with fundamental differences from any other generations he had ever encountered in his academic career. Digital natives had "spent their entire lives surrounded by and using computers, video games, digital music players, video cams, cell phones, and all the other toys and tools of the digital age" (Prensky 2001, p. 1).

Digital natives were born later than 1980 and raised in a technology-oriented environment. They cannot recall childhood memories without using some technology. This generation demonstrates remarkable adjustment skills to any new gadget and innovation that hits the market (Papakonstantinidis 2014). The early digital natives had firsthand experience with the personal computer boom and the rapid development of video game consoles from Spectrum, Amstrad, and Amiga to the fancy Playstation and Xbox series. They got fascinated by the World Wide Web and its potential, such as sending e-mails, chatting online, placing video calls, using mobile devices, and communicating via social networking sites.

The digital natives who were born in the early 1980s have grown up experimenting a lot with technology. Some of them became entrepreneurs taking advantage of the countless opportunities the Internet provides. They explored the possibilities of online communication and saw great opportunities for entertainment, information, education, and personal engagement with technology. Facebook's founder Mark Zuckerberg or Google's founders Larry Page and Sergey Brin became multibillionaires at a very young age due to their innovative ideas that shaped today's online environment. Nowadays, college students or just self-taught programmers are dreaming of coming up with the next best idea that will do what Steve Jobs and Bill Gates started almost three decades ago.

Digital natives demonstrate a natural inclination toward technology and electronic devices. The generation gap, seen as an intrinsic factor in the labor history, is advanced as the current generation of online users demonstrate high adaptability to anything new. This behavior is in stark contrast to their parents and grandparents, classified within the genre of social media as digital immigrants (Prensky 2001). Digital immigrants are experienced online users who, although they manage to catch up with technology quickly, are still not considered full-fledged "members" of the hashtag generation.

Digital natives are especially adept at functioning within an online environment, whether this is a web-based or a mobile interface. When it comes to a business setting, digital natives are especially predisposed to this sociological profile. Configured by e-mail and instant messaging communications, collaborative project management (wikis), and virtual meetings through Skype or WhatsApp, digital natives find validation in their professional standing by way of multiple digital accounts. Digital natives are first-generation bloggers, vloggers, wiki contributors, online gaming community (clan) leaders, and top influencers on social networking sites. Many of those same digital natives might also have an avatar (digital self) that lives in virtual worlds and online games like Lineage and World of Warcraft (Qualman 2009).

Digital natives are equally eager to test any new gadget as soon as it hits the market. The iPhone, the Samsung Galaxy, and other smartphones or wearable devices are an evidence of this movement. Nowadays, digital natives listen to music through streaming platforms such as Spotify and Deezer. They most probably own not more than a few songs, as they claim that "everything is on YouTube and Spotify." Digital natives get informed via social media and the accounts they follow. They like reading titles than full articles. The transition to the professional world is coming naturally to digital natives who from their youth aim at what Tapscott and Williams (2008) call organic connectivity. This means that this generation of college graduates is more open to set up professional networks and establish connections than their parents. In fact, digital natives have been connecting with people based on similar interests from the beginning of their interaction with technology.

The first digital natives have grown up, completed their college, and are entering the business world. With such openness and diversity in business models (i.e., Microsoft Office 365, Google Docs, Skype for Business, GoToMeetings, VoiceThread, etc.), digital natives can run web-based start-ups before their graduation. The digital world offers countless opportunities to young entrepreneurs to make a living from home, by using online resources such as blogs, vlogs, content sites, SEO consultancy, web design, and graphic design. Also, the new digital professional landscape offers a variety of new types of remote jobs via websites such as Flexjobs, We Work Remotely, Skip the Drive, Landing Jobs, and AngelList.

With the rapid proliferation of social media in everyday life and business, the next generation of digital natives has turned to become social natives. In 2014, Marc Foulger posted to Hootsuite's blog an article titled "Meet the First Generation of Social Natives" to introduce the term. Foulger (2014) writes that social media is like home to social natives. They spend all day checking their social accounts, looking for hashtag trends, and sharing content nonstop. Social natives are members of a multichannel generation that enthusiastically adopts new platforms that older generations such as millennials and Gen Xer's discover later. Snapchat is an example of a social media application; Gen Xer's rejected it, but social natives loved it.

Social natives are much more than trendsetters. They think, consume, discuss, and collaborate differently. Elon University professor Janna Anderson argues that people born after 2000 tend to be always online as they "have grown up in a world that has come to offer them instant access to nearly the entirety of human knowledge, and incredible opportunities to connect, create and collaborate" (Foulger 2014). Social natives do not seem to adopt the old digital habits of the previous digital generations. Although e-mail is still a primary communication tool, social natives will mostly rely on messaging apps such as WhatsApp or Facebook Messenger to call their friends and colleagues. Even Skype seems old-fashioned to them. New-generation social media users prefer sending direct messages (they call them DM) to other people's inboxes, rather than e-mailing them. Many of the social natives do not need to get someone's phone number anymore. All they need is the person's account on Snapchat, and they will stay connected.

Social natives comfortably shift among various online platforms and mobile applications. They do not merely rely on a single network as the "always on" concept matters the most to them. These young people have also developed a new business mindset that everyone can be a celebrity and can quickly succeed in their careers. Some of the pioneers of such a business mindset are Facebook's founder Mark Zuckerberg and Google's founders Larry Page and Sergey Brin, showing that billionaire status can be attained at a very early stage in next-generation careers. These technology innovators conceived a great idea, managed it well to dominate a specific online category, and then brought it to fruition as initial public offerings at the right time.

The social natives' business mindset developed one more major change. Social natives realized that they do not have to be technology geniuses to become rich and famous. Social media opened tremendous opportunities to every single user to go online and share his/her passion with the world. If people like what they see, they will see it again and again. They will also share it with their friends. That is how someone's passion for fashion, music, movies, and much more becomes viral.

Social natives demonstrate a unique understanding of technology since they were children. This rare knowledge has had a significant impact on cultural forms as well as product segmentation, as this generation seems to appreciate diversity and change in both education and business (Zur and Zur 2011). For example, similar to digital natives, the social natives have a different meaning of lifelong learning. To them, education is a collaborative process that all they have to do is to search on Google and YouTube for the most relevant results to find their answers.

Experience-driven and multitasking-savvy, the new hashtag generation of employees and entrepreneurs are horizontal in efficacy and practice (Prensky 2001). This book aims to explain how this age of social natives is preparing for the leap from school to work. Will they look for a job or will they first try to create their professional opportunities? The question that arises in most studies is to what extent the current business world is open enough to accept and fulfill the hashtag generation's expectations.

Recruiting the Social Natives

Knowledge of the typical behaviors of the hashtag generation forces companies to adopt new strategies and practices to recruit and retain the most talented social natives. As automation gradually replaces manufacturing, businesses rely heavily on finding the most innovative employees who live on the fringe of the digital and physical world. The trend in recruitment is innovation as organizations should consider the new twists in the business landscape.

The competition to hire the very best candidates remains strong and complicated. Modern organizations aim to adapt to innovative social and business trends to attract the new generation of professionals. Certainly, that is the message that emerges loud and clear from social natives in certain critical studies in the field of social recruitment and personal branding. This chapter offers a brief outline of personality traits of jobseekers, which reflect the four core values for recruitment of new hires as originally described by Yeaton (2008) and simplified by Papakonstantinidis (2017) as shown in the following table.

Personality Traits of the New Generation

1. Strong sense of morality	They express their concern about the current economic situation in the world. They do not want to give up and not pursue a satisfying career pathway. The current situation made them more mature as they redefined what is essential and what is unnecessary. What these people seek from their future employers is honesty, vision, and stability. They appreciate hard work, and now they are more cautious than ever not to make the same mistakes their parents' generations did.
2. Goal and achievement oriented	They seek new challenges, and they are not afraid of changing careers and jobs if their needs and ambitions are not satisfied. They dream to start their own startup company using the Internet's power to make a living by doing what they like. They are goal oriented, and they want to achieve in their lives, anywhere in the world. They see no boundaries to pursue their professional career.

3. Technology natives	They use computers and mobile phones all the time. The lines between personal and professional lives are blurred. They start by playing games, and they want to experience any new technology and trend that they are aware of. The current economic situation is not seen as a problem, but rather as an opportunity for online entrepreneurship. Unlike their parents, digital natives do not seek standardized employment (Prensky 2001). Instead, they are far more likely to opt to start their careers as pampered information or technological employees or as self-employed online entrepreneurs (Manafy and Gautschi 2011). Digital natives also work ubiquitous hours and in random locations. Most indicate that freedom from workspace limitations lends to productivity.
4. Value intelligence and innovation without workplace restrictions	Social natives want to become the leaders of change in their countries. They seek for employers who are open to new experiences. They aim for intelligence and innovation in their workplace. They can work from home as they feel that a typical office might be quite restricting to develop their creative side.

(Papakonstantinidis 2017)

Multiple virtues and skills are to be found in the hashtag generation. Social natives adopt business approaches far less complicated than the current ones. They possess technological nous in abundance to design and implement a low-budget plan, by using the power of social media to talk to their customers. Despite the general notion that anyone who spends all day on social media is lazy and apathetic, social natives are hard-working and efficient as long as they find the meaning in what they do. If they are provided with the appropriate motivational tools and rewards, they can offer substantial assistance and intelligence to any business.

Let us not lose sight. Social natives have distinct differences from the previous generations. A new taxonomy categorizes jobseekers and career opportunists as follows: Denials, Socializers, Contributors, and Achievers (Papakonstantinidis 2014).

A Taxonomy of Digital Jobseekers

1. Denials

Even though they were born into the digital era, some skilled and well-educated people do not gravitate comfortably toward technology. Moreover, by comparison with a majority of their fellow Gen Yers, they are not addicted to social media, the ubiquitous use of texting, or mobile devices. Of course, they have a smartphone, an e-mail address, and most probably an account on Facebook, but not on other social networking sites. They tend to be more skeptical toward technology and its effects on privacy. This category understands that technology is here to stay and attempts to use it to the lowest possible degree, primarily when they understand that they have little choice but to do so.

A manifestation of this is using Google to unearth some data on a particular site before venturing into it. Owning an account on Facebook is possible, although it is one they may not access on a daily basis. Moreover, instead of finding the location of a particular place on, for instance, Google Maps, they will ask directions to it. If they must, they will go on Skype or employ a GPS system, but with little enthusiasm. When it comes to employment, the denials will reject any idea of 24/7 online connectivity with colleagues and employers.

2. Socializers

This category comprises the bulk of the social native population. Socializers almost live on social media enjoying and thriving on technology and its various gadgets. Mainly they use their high-tech mobile devices that are connected to a power bank to maximize battery life. They watch videos on YouTube, instead of mainstream TV programs or films. When information is needed—no matter what kind—their first port of call is always Google. It is more challenging to make these young people answer their phone than it is to get a message to them through an online medium or by posting a video on Snapchat. They live for immediate, fluid communication and typically own a portable digital device that provides 24/7 web connectivity.

Socializers typically prefer sending a text over an e-mail and might be a little less willing than its seniors to compose written material coherently. Socializers are passionate contributors and online gamers. These people will wait for days to purchase the latest i[product]. For them, technology is enjoyable, and its most recent developments are of great interest. Socializers are motivated by gamification elements at work, aiming to receive more digital points or to become the office's "mayor" based on how many check-ins they clicked.

3. **Contributors**

This category of web users feels that technology is what defines them. They are well-versed social media users who started early on, and now they have evolved into active bloggers. They see the Internet as a tool to make a living. They are in constant search of the next best idea that will bring them money and glory. Ideals drive contributors as they believe in free circulation of ideas, and they want to express their opinion openly.

They believe Facebook is too childish and annoying. Contributors, in contrast, see Twitter and Instagram as the most interesting social media platforms they can use. For them, Twitter is bright, immediate, democratic, and fun. Instagram and Pinterest are more sophisticated, thoughtful, and excellent sources of inspiration. Contributors recognize the importance of social media in providing professional opportunities, and only recently they realized they could use it to promote their online persona. They are positive when their company allows free access to social media.

(*continued*)

4. **Achievers**

This category of social natives sees technology as a tool to develop their career. They are goal oriented, which makes them careful with what they post and where. The achievers show a robust primary motivation, and they use any possible means to achieve their objectives. They treat social media mainly professionally and conscientiously.

They primarily use LinkedIn and Pinterest to contribute to the social media community. They participate in LinkedIn groups, and they try to post content only relevant to their field of interest. They also like Pinterest, to create boards of inspiration to connect with people who share the same interests. Achievers want to try new social media applications as long as they see the potential to add the extra value to their overall profile. They will most probably rate their social influence on Klout, or they will participate in academic discussions on Quora if they recognize its importance to their digital image. Achievers are afraid of bad comments. They do not want to have anything that might harm their digital reputation.

Achievers are also keen on mobile technologies. They own a smartphone, and they use it as an icon of status and prestige. They set up strategies, and they keep their CVs up-to-date for any available business opportunity. Whether they work or not, achievers are in constant search to take on new professional experience. They are not loyal to one company as they can see other available positions to compare and contrast for their benefit. Just as contributors, achievers request full social media access from their employers.

Papakonstantinidis (2014)

Modern organizations aim toward the integration of intelligent software system applications online in their recruitment strategy. Tomorrow's employees will have to mobilize their work and perform in both the offline and the online worlds. Job auction websites such as Freelancer.com, Guru.com, and Odesk.com offer alternative opportunities to regular employment. The more connected such web-sites are with social media, the more opportunities they offer to job candidates. Social natives receive job alerts from Google, Twitter, and LinkedIn. They can also arrange to receive customized job alerts via e-mail through Glassdoor and other job portals by adding details such as job title/keyword and location. Then job portals could recommend jobs based on past searches and other criteria that matter to the job candidate (salary, company reviews, and tasks). The online world of-fers a variety of connected applications in laptops, smartphones, tablets, and other wearable devices. From this standpoint, the future of virtual recruitment appears limitless.

Social Nativity and the Limitless Opportunities

This chapter discussed the social native's profile. For social natives, money is not the only criterion when searching for their career oppor-tunities. An open organizational culture that provides flexible working conditions and unlimited access to social media is equally important. Young people do not mind working during weekends or nights. They want to work on their mobile phones and laptops, without feeling bound to a 9-to-5 work schedule. They follow a wide variety of mul-timedia sources, being keen on parallel learning and multitasking. The social natives treat today's workplace environment as *phygital*, both physical and digital.

The new phygital workplace environment directs new approaches and strategies. Social nativity offers limitless opportunities to people who switch workplaces and careers during their professional life easier than ever before. Jobvite's (2018) whitepaper titled "The New Model for Modern Recruiting: Continuous Candidate Engagement Engage Candidates from First Look to First Day" discusses a new model for modern recruiting strategies. The Jobvite authors argue that the rules of job searching and recruiting have radically changed due to social media and other interactive digital communication platforms. They highlight the following eight trends to be considered by recruiters in the future:

The Talent Crunch Is Getting Worse

If you're not in the talent crunch yet, you will be. The unemployment rate has dropped to a 17-year low of 4.1 percent, meaning that almost every qualified candidate is already employed. And the hunt for skilled talent is only getting more challenging. In fact, according to the 2017 Recruiter Nation Report, 89 percent of recruiters think it will get more competitive, and only 2 percent think it will get less competitive.

Candidates Are More Informed, Have More Choices

As companies struggle to find workers to fill record-high job openings, candidates pick companies, not vice versa—particularly educated, skilled talent who can pick and choose from plenty of options. But don't discount hourly workers; they do their homework too and are informed about where the jobs are and are always looking for ways to increase their take-home pay.

The Up-and-Coming Workforce Has Different Expectations

Millennials will comprise more than one in three adult Americans by 2020, and 75 percent of the workforce by 2025. Whether it's millennials, Gen Z, or the generations that follow, it is critical to rethink your recruiting strategy to be able to reach these younger candidates in the way they want to be communicated with, and with clear branding that speaks to their values. If you make them click too many times, or your campaign doesn't work on mobile, you're going to lose them.

Candidates Will Reject You Preemptively

Job-hopping is the new normal, especially for the up-and-coming workforce. The content that is most important to jobseekers researching a company includes employer reviews (at 37 percent), and after that, textual content on a company website (at 24 percent), as well as company publications or products. If they're turned off by reviews or can't find what they're looking for, they'll move on, rejecting you before you even know they're looking. That's even true when it comes to your current employees—staying at a company for less than 3 years is the new norm.

Anyone Can Be Found by Anyone

As of April 2017, LinkedIn passed the 500 million user mark, and Facebook was over 2 billion. Thanks to social media, it's easier than ever to find candidates on social media—easier for you and for everyone else.

Jobs Are Fluid

In one study of 1,000 U.S. office workers, one-third had a second job and more than half (56 percent) predicted we would all have multiple jobs in the future. Increasingly, work is distributed across geographies; people are choosing part-time, project-based work; and many have side gigs—44 million according to one report. In this gig economy, fluid work arrangements call for flexible hiring strategies.

Speed Is the New Currency

Moving quickly on candidates is the name of the game. They're always seeking and you're always hiring, so you better move fast if you want to keep those top candidates. Many companies give candidates offer letters on the day they interview, before they even leave the office. Rising innovations in screening—such as text interviewing, chatbots, and on-demand video—take days, if not weeks, out of the process, helping recruiters find top talent faster than ever before.

A Signed Offer Is No Longer the Finish Line

The signed offer is an important milestone, but not the finish line. Even after a candidate has signed, he/she can still decide not to join your company. There's even a good chance he/she will change his/her mind if he/she doesn't find it satisfactory: Over one-quarter of employees are willing to quit a new job in the first 90 days, leaving you to start over again.

Jobvite (2018)

The rules of recruitment are changing indeed. Social natives aim for flexible work conditions to allow them to develop new professional skills. Although social natives seek for career stability, they keep an eye on their LinkedIn profiles to be ready for their next adventure. For the new breed of employees, social media is a way of living and doing business. The online environment offers limitless opportunities that can be seen by the social natives as the new El Dorado of social and online entrepreneurship.

With the rapid proliferation of instant messaging applications such as WhatsApp, Viber, and Messenger, our phone becomes an essential tool to connect us with our colleagues. Social natives live in a new digital culture, which has its language, etiquette, and rituals. Social natives are willing to post personal information on social media without thinking of maintaining and protecting their privacy. They want to connect with their friends and family. To that extent, social natives work on their professional image starting from their digital footprint.

Job hunters in digital nativity would start by setting an account on LinkedIn and building their professional network. As they would have done before buying any new device, social natives would look online for company reviews and additional information on Google and Quora. If the job requires, most social natives will enjoy producing a short video resume to demonstrate their skills. They would have no problem sharing their thoughts to Facebook groups like "Work It Daily" to seek advice from other group members.

For social natives, training and induction should be fun. They are seeking organizations that are engaging their employees most transparently. They do not want to stay in the shadows. Social natives believe that learning should take place anywhere and anytime through teambuilding games, social intranets, and fun gatherings. Social natives will not hesitate to seek professional solutions by asking their online friends. Not all companies are ready to accept such a breach of information. Nevertheless, the companies that will try to restrict social natives' access to the web will have a hard time to recruit or even to retain the best talents for an extended period.

Corporate social media policies should establish a standard approach to help people clarify the lines between personal and professional information. The new corporate world should renew its plans to include digital safety concerns. Companies should be able to address issues such as spamming colleagues, revealing corporate data, posting inappropriate pictures online, digital stalking and harassment, and bullying online. Social natives should know that the new digital culture comes with great excitement and great responsibility.

The next chapter will discuss the concept of social recruiting. What do companies seek from their candidates? Do HR managers screen job applicants by checking their social media accounts? Does social recruiting shape a new reality in human resources management? Let's find out.

CHAPTER 4

Recruiting in the Brave New Online Social World

This chapter at a glance:

- Recruiting 2.0
- Social recruiting and its impact on society
- The brave new online world
- The new El Dorado of jobseekers
- Networking as a cornerstone of graduate job pursuit
- Gamification in recruitment
- Personal thoughts on social recruiting

Justin Bieber

Real Name: Justin Bieber

Country: Canada

Social Media: YouTube

His Story: Justin Bieber owes every inch of his fame and fortune to YouTube, which was how Usher discovered him and catapulted him to the stars. His mother would record him singing and dancing and upload the videos to YouTube. She intended to share them with friends and family. However, Bieber got the attention of millions. After Usher discovered him, he flew him to the USA and the rest is history. The young superstar is under 30 years old and holds a fortune of approximately 200 million dollars!

(James 2018)

Recruiting 2.0

New technologies have changed human communication and professional collaboration. To name a few of the changes, people can now work remotely from home, set up companies just by using their computer, and offer services to people who they never meet in person. Such technologies, and especially the development of online job portals and online social networks, have radically changed the labor market landscape and the overall recruitment and selection process. Today, people set up their professional accounts on social media such as LinkedIn and Xing to attract headhunters and recruiters. Also, employers do not wait until they receive a good CV and application. As soon as they identify a unique talent, employers can reach the employee directly and make a job offer. Just in the fourth quarter of 2016, 67 percent of unemployed and 61 percent of employed workers in the age group of 16 to 24 years used the Internet to either seek for an online job vacancy on job portals or visit a professional social networking website in the previous month (Domkundwar 2017).

The leading website in professional networking is LinkedIn. A LinkedIn study highlighted the importance of Big Data to recruit and retain the talents in the labor market (Domkundwar 2017). The use of Big Data in recruitment is one of the top trends in human resources management (HRM). In Chapter 6, we discuss more thoroughly about Big Data and People Analytics in recruitment. The same study revealed that approximately 72 percent of modern and multinational organizations comprehend the importance of fully digitalizing their HR processes. It is no secret anymore that almost 90 percent of multinational corporations, as well as 40 percent of small and medium enterprises in the United States, are using social networking websites to hire people.

Job recruiters in U.S.-based companies admit that due to the use of social media the results were very satisfying (Jobvite 2018). The numbers and statistics are even more impressive. Hiring decision-makers argue that the implementation of social media in the hiring process will further develop to test the applicants not only based on their credentials but also based on the strength of their professional networks. On the other hand, jobseekers play a key role in the new digital HR landscape. Jobseekers tend to self-promote their skills and qualifications to attract the best companies. The Internet cultivated the notion that anyone can work anywhere in the world. Today, it seems that jobseekers have the power to decide on their next employer. This was not so easy in the past when professional opportunities were limited. Nowadays, the application for a job can require just one click. LinkedIn or Glassdoor users can apply directly from the online platform by clicking the "Apply" button and sending their social media account to recruiters.

Is there a downside to all this? Of course there is. Social media shed light on both sides of the hiring process. On the one hand, companies can now decide who to hire based on a candidate's overall digital reputation and an online background check. For example, provocative or inappropriate content, and photographs, videos, or text that can be associated with a candidate might potentially affect the final hiring decision. On the other hand, candidates use a variety of online resources to find information about a company that until recently was considered confidential, such as salary ranges, interview questions, internal reviews, and images from the corporate premises.

Today's corporate world is more digital than ever before. The new breed of employees are the social natives who demonstrate a natural inclination toward new technologies and social media. Companies aim to recruit the talents that will offer them an advantage over their competitors. This chapter aims to discuss the concept of social recruiting and its applications in the next generation of both the hiring managers and jobseekers. First, let's examine the impact of social recruitment on modern society.

Social Recruiting and Its Impact on Society

The primary objective of social media was to mediate our social interactions. Since inception, social media has affected the behavior of online users as to how to communicate with friends, make new friends, get informed, and share links with the public (Boyd and Ellison 2008). Nowadays, we have a variety of virtual communication channels ranging from e-mail, instant messengers, video chat platforms, virtual group communication platforms, and (micro) blogging services. Gmail threads, Snapchat messages, Instagram posts, Tweets, Facebook updates, WhatsApp groups, and Skype calls are some of the most famous forms of virtual communication. Also, social natives prefer playing online games and connecting with people who share the same passion for games such as Call of Duty (CoD), FIFA, Lineage, Grand Theft Auto (GTA), and World of Warcraft (WoW).

The high-speed Internet connection, the abundance of computer-mediated communication platforms, and the adoption of mobile devices are the main reasons for satisfying our need to communicate and publicly express our identity. Today we use the social media to interact with other online users, follow the news, watch our favorite TV shows, listen to streamed music, and do business. Social natives rely on their online friend networks to get informed and entertained. Traditional newspapers and magazines are not their primary source of information. Social natives follow blogs and social media accounts on Twitter and Instagram. It is a common practice for several news websites to allow their users to comment on their stories. Usually, the user comments are becoming more important than the actual story.

The Internet impacted the business world as well. Digitization affected marketing, project management, human resources, and all other business sectors. Marketers argue that the new technologies allow them to target their audiences and customize their services. Project managers use the Internet to collaborate with all stakeholders at once through web platforms such as GoToMeeting and Skype for Business. HR managers use corporate websites, online job portals, and social media to look for candidates and recruit the best talents in a faster and more accurate manner.

The business world is now more open and flexible to adopt new practices than ever before. Nevertheless, intellectual property and liability concerns form a continuum in social recruiting audit of postings, as corporate brands must be subject to rigorous identity management online during the job-posting period. Modern organizations need to be brave and bold to accept online criticism as well as praise. Online users can comment either positively or negatively on the job vacancy or on aspects relevant to the company's reputation, such as payment conditions, reliability, work environment, and other factors, that until recently were considered confidential information. Are all organizations ready to enter the brave new online social world?

The Brave New Online Social World

The brave new online social world is a unique environment where people interact, work, entertain, and learn. The Internet is the context and not merely a tool with limitless content (Hooley 2012). With the use of social media, the lines between personal and public life are blurred. People seem to be more open to exposing their private moments, having a flawed understanding about what type of information is public and what is private. Also, sociologists examine the notion that the Internet is the most democratic tool of communication, showing evidence of the opposite by addressing the issue of the digital divide.

In the brave new online social world, people search for everything. The leading online search engine, Google, processes over 40,000 search queries every second on average, which translates to over 3.5 billion searches per day and 1.2 trillion searches per year worldwide. The Internet has become ubiquitous. Personal computers or laptops are not the only devices that allow people to connect online. They used to but not anymore. Users can access the web using mobile devices as well. New technologies and computer trends such as Machine Deep Learning (MDL), Digital Currencies, Blockchains, Robotics, and the Internet of Things (IoT) are already available in the market. Electronics, artificial intelligence (AI) software, sensors, actuators, and GPS trackers are embedded in various clothing and casual accessories. Such technologies and IoT devices include driverless vehicles, home automation, wearable technology, health monitors, and AI personal assistants.

It is also evident to recognize the social change in how people organize their files, using cloud computing services, asking search engines for anything, wondering "Who they are" or "What to vote," among other personal search queries. There are more than 1 billion search queries posted on Google every day. Google reports that 15 percent of the searches every day has never been done in the past. In 2010, Google introduced autocomplete, which allows the search engine to suggest instantly what we are about to type. All we have to do is to type in the first letters of a word, then Google will complete the rest of the search query based on past and frequent global queries. Since then the autocomplete feature has resulted in some pretty interesting results. For instance, if you start typing "what would happen if..." the query can bring the most unexpected results, such as "what would happen if the sun exploded?" or "what would happen if there was no moon?" People ask Google to find them a job, to help them with their relationships, or to assist them in changing their lives. There is a great need for people to ask Google for some advice on their branding as well.

According to a Pew Internet Center's study on social trust, the level of people's faith toward information they retrieve online increases steadily (Rainie and Anderson 2017). People use Wikipedia as an educational tool, check on Yelp for opinions and peer recommendations, go online for medical issues, and trust Twitter as a more valid source of information than traditional media. People also use the Internet for recreational purposes. Online games, web-based music applications, online purchases, and downloads of files are all examples of online social behavior. With the rapid proliferation of e-commerce, scholars now examine the implications of the so-called online currency, Bitcoin, to ascertain whether or not it can contribute to the actual economy.

As a new social phenomenon, social recruiting has to be studied both from a sociological and from a business perspective. Currently, the term "social recruiting" has become a buzzword in the business world since online technologies and social networking websites are offering new opportunities to HR managers and recruiters to get in touch with candidates in niche communities, engage with them, inform them, and recruit the best talent. Reviewing candidates' profiles on social media appears to be a useful tool for HR managers. When HR managers come across a "clean" candidate's profile, they tend to positively consider the candidate in contrast to those whose online profiles demonstrate poor communication skills or show evidence of misbehavior (talking negatively about previous employers and inappropriate images).

The El Dorado for Jobseekers

In today's work environment, organizations compete on several fronts, including profits, market share, innovation, and talent recruitment and retention. According to Jobvite's 2016 Recruiter Nation Survey, "in the midst of a growing gig economy, the threat of job automation, and electoral shifts, 44% of jobseekers are optimistic for what's to come." Here are some of the research findings that we find interesting:

- Jobseekers have mixed feelings about the job market—but most are always open to the prospect of a new job.
- As much as 74 percent of employees are open to a new job.
- About 39 percent report that it is more difficult to find a new job this year than last year, while 19 percent find it easier. Social media is a powerful tool in the job search, and Facebook has the upper hand.
- Social media is pervasive. As much as 67 percent of social media jobseekers use Facebook; only 35 percent use Twitter.
- Meanwhile, 59 percent use social media to research the company culture of organizations they are interested in. From health care to parental leave, we find mixed reports on perks and benefits.
- Health care is the most common perk, with 43 percent of jobseekers reporting that they receive health care coverage as part of their job.
- Almost a fifth of jobseekers polled have held a gig-type job—through companies like Airbnb or Uber—and 56 percent of those respondents report that this has been their main source of income.
- As much as 55 percent of jobseekers are at least a bit concerned about job obsolescence.
- Despite these concerns, many jobseekers (44 percent) are optimistic about their job prospects in the long run.

(Jobvite 2016)

Jobvite's (2016) study highlights that when it comes to the recruitment and selection of employees, the traditional recruitment practices rank second to social networking websites such as LinkedIn and Glassdoor. Virtual job fairs, Facebook, Twitter posts for jobs, and many online fora and niche job websites are shaping a new labor market landscape. Social natives are more likely to accept employment offers that allow freedom of expression from the outset in the social networking sites (SNS) environment and include perks such as flexible work relations and remote mobility, in contrast to the traditional job offers with an emphasis on aspects such as safety, salary, and professional potential.

Networking and Graduate Job Pursuit

Networking refers to connections among strangers, whereas people "network" with those they know. The term *networking* is often defined as "individuals' attempts to develop and maintain relationships with others who have the potential to assist them in their work or career" (Forret and Dougherty 2001, p. 284). When it comes to online networking, one cannot separate the digital from the physical world. Nevertheless, in the brave new online social world, visibility prefaces performance. The quintessential ticket to profit and power in contemporary professional circles provides unlimited and unexplored opportunities for a graduate's entry into the job market (Yeung 2009).

There are many social networking websites available online. While some target specific demographic segments, the attention to designated clusters and communities is multiscale and can often vary in response to membership interests. One can recognize distinct differences between confidential memberships (professional associations), online environments that allow public observation and participation (Facebook), and representation of professional identity in a more "business-focused" setting (LinkedIn).

Before the advent of the Internet, recruitment was a vertical business process, comprising a value chain commencing at the point of administration and concluding in the hire of a candidate. Today, the HRM recruitment process entails a more passive mode of recruitment, one that involves a wide range of liaisons, from social networking websites and spin-offs of traditional vehicles such as local press to online job portals. With the extensive penetration of social networking websites, the recruiting process is now more engaging from both sides than before.

Partnership with SimplyHired.com, an intelligent, abductive search source for traditional job posts, increases the volume of opportunities available to candidates through the site. Membership of LinkedIn puts potential employees or consultants into contact with companies and groups that might lead to a contract or hire. Requisite profile creation by members at the time of joining reduces formerly time-consuming tasks in CV presentation and initiation of a connection with others in the network. Add social media buttons to personal and professional e-mail signatures and other online website sources, one's professional identity is exposed to an entire panoply of recruitment opportunities waiting to be filled.

The change in the HRM recruitment process has been widely discussed in management scholarship, which posits the benefits and the drawbacks associated with the practice. One issue for recruiters is the time capsule control on sites and adequate screening for current availability of candidates who promote themselves via social media. In a simple search for candidates on LinkedIn, for example, the recruiter might end up finding a large number of well-qualified individuals who meet the criteria but are not currently available.

Varied introduction to social media applications also may impact on recruitment evaluation in ways that do not necessarily select candidates with the best-matched skill set based on manipulation of site tools. Some candidates are skillful enough to post streaming visual aids alongside their CV (video resumes, personal websites) and other standard documents such as portfolios and sample works. For this reason, those who oppose social recruiting argue that online profiles raise ethical concerns. Online profiles cannot be an accurate representation of a candidate's skills and credentials, as many online users can deceive the recruiter with false information. Also, the issue of personal and confidential information raises discussions around security, especially identity theft. Finally, since the modern social networking websites can offer recruiters the option to filter online profiles based on demographic characteristics and physical appearance, candidates might feel discriminated against the hiring process.

Employers can use social media to filter out everyone who does not fit designated "subjective" factors, such as the school they attended or their past professional experience. It is evident that social networks can potentially harm the recruitment process and, therefore, a company's reliability. To avoid such unethical practices, LinkedIn allows its users to lock down or even temporarily disable their online profiles, in case they are not currently seeking any professional opportunities. Nevertheless, only a few do it.

Social recruiting has undoubtedly brought a different kind of labor market debate to the fore. New social network rules on confidential corporate and member information can, at times, be released online.

Although corporate espionage is more prevalent than ever, the focus on risk management in this area is progressively a standard where vulnerabilities pose a threat to company's profit and its employees. Advancement of online ethical best practices through a site membership agreement is part of the recent focus in both academic and professional literature on the topic. The need to examine both the advantages and disadvantages of global social networking websites as they present themselves in the recruitment process also emerges in this research.

As the current business environment has begun to shrink and has become more competitive and demanding, graduates struggle to find a job that is both satisfying and relevant to their academic credentials. Approximately 83 percent of companies in the United States seek candidates using SNS, and about 46 percent agree that they have the intention to invest in social recruitment processes (Jobvite 2016). Access to a virtual marketplace of "passive" and "alert" candidates allows organizations to employ this new method of recruitment as a cost-cutting mechanism within HRM budgeting. Social media reduces the number of per diem hours required to locate suitable candidates to 4 hours for each candidate.

Although social networking websites do not substitute for all established aspects of recruiting, employers have been responsive to the platform standard of a portfolio and summary as an initial solicitation of interest. In earlier renditions of online job portals such as Monster.com and Careerbuilder.com, candidates appear alongside organizations so that quality control of communications interface in HRM transmission is streamlined to eliminate tiresome steps in the application and review processes.

The brave new online social world introduces us to many different aspects of recruitment. First, we had the proliferation of the general online job portals. Then we had the niche job websites and the development of the social networking websites that affected the labor market landscape. Is this all? Next, we discuss the development of gamification in recruitment as an alternative method to recruit and select the best talents in the market.

Gamification in Recruitment

The quest to recruit the best talents in the market is getting more challenging than ever. In their effort to win the battle and bring the best possible employees in the organization, HR managers added several game elements in the recruiting process. Social natives love online games on gaming platforms such as PlayStation and Xbox. This generation of new college graduates is willing to join in competitive virtual arenas where the best wins. Therefore, employers use virtual games in their recruiting strategies, by integrating reward points, virtual badges, special opts, quests, and role-playing games.

For example, the administration of PricewaterhouseCoopers (PwC) in Hungary initiated a 12-day online simulation game called Multipoly to recruit college students. The game required students to use their Facebook accounts to play. Participants had to deal with actual job tasks and solve real-life accounting issues. The accounting and consulting firm's experts provided students with quarterly goals and responsibilities as they would do to entry-level employees. At the end of the 12-day simulation game, the winner who met the goals was given a contract at PwC. Noemi Biro, PwC's recruitment leader in Hungary, argued that the game boosted employer branding, strengthened the firm's professional network, and provided participants with auditing and consulting insights in a fun and engaging way.

Gamification in recruitment triggers people's interest. Gamification adds the sense of competition and reward that makes people more engaged and willing to win. Also, employers get a clearer picture of each candidate's skills and potential. It appears that gamification in recruitment is a win–win situation. The examples of companies that used gamification in their internal business processes are many. Deloitte implemented gamification to recruit talented employees by requesting them to make reasonable decisions to get through a virtual forest. NTT Data initiated an internal communication gamification platform to evaluate its employees' leadership abilities. Another consulting firm, Bluewolf, launched the program Going Social to increase interaction between its employees and the market experts.

One might say that gamification applies to computer and consulting companies. Not quite. Gamification has several applications in almost every business sector. Marriott International initiated a recruiting game called My Marriott Hotel to attract young employees. Millennials had to use Facebook to start managing a hotel restaurant kitchen. Players had to budget everything, order virtual goods, make business decisions, hire people, train employees, and serve clients. Imagine playing the famous online game, The Sims, but this time the winner gets a contract to work for Marriott. All other participants who earned virtual points get badges that can function as future work referrals.

The beauty company L'Oreal initiates every year a brand competition called Brandstorm to spot young talents in marketing. Groups of university students from all over the world participate in the Brandstorm to receive the company's brief to launch an innovative product. Gamification is a modern talent acquisition strategy. Such gamified tools have been used by companies to attract millennials and increase employer branding. With the continuous advancements in technology, more gamified recruiting ideas will hit the market. The integration of gamification tools with virtual reality and augmented reality technologies might shape a new battleground in both personal branding and recruitment.

Personal Thoughts on Social Recruiting

As online social networks become widely known across online users, organizations are shifting their attention to social networking websites and blogs to perform a wide range of business activities. This chapter discussed how companies integrate the use of social networking websites in internal communication practices and HRM.

Social natives require unrestricted access to social media and transparency that was once unavailable to job candidates. Social recruiting involves both sides, recruiter and jobseeker, in the decision-making process. As companies conduct personnel searches, potential candidates gain insight into organizational benefits that may be compatible with career goals and employment objectives (Moses 2009).

The rapid growth of technology develops new recruitment strategies that add game elements in the process. Gamification, social recruitment, virtual reality, and augmented reality will play a vital role in future recruitment. This chapter aimed to shed light both on the opportunities and the threats that social recruiting might create, by examining both sides—the career seekers and the recruiters. Today's corporate world expects *no more lies*. If we want to introduce our brand new self, we should embrace transparency.

CHAPTER 5

The Brand New Me

This chapter at a glance:

- Getting SoLoMo ready
- Start your brand strategy early on
- Google yourself
- Remove information you do not want public
- Stories to get you hired through social media
- Stories to get you fired through social media
- Our brand ecosystem

Michelle Phan

Origin: Vietnamese-American

Social Media: YouTube

Her Story: Michelle Phan is a cosmetics entrepreneur who got her start giving makeup application tutorials on YouTube in 2007. In 2011, she told Forbes that she took her inspiration from that painter of happy little trees, the late television painting instructor Bob Ross. Her methods brought her to the attention of Lancôme, the French cosmetics giant, which made her their official video makeup artist in 2010 after seeing her feature their products in her videos. In 2012 she started the subscription cosmetics service Ipsy, and in 2013, L'Oreal created a makeup line for her called "em." This year, she graced the "30 Under 30" lists of both Inc. and Forbes.

Michelle Phan went from growing up on food stamps to building a nearly $100 million empire. And it all started on YouTube.

(continued)

Michelle Phan, 27, is an American woman we can all admire. She is the first woman to reach 1 billion views on YouTube. She now has nearly 9 million followers.

Her "how to" makeup videos have become so successful that she's parlayed their popularity into her own L'Oreal makeup line, cofounded the company Ipsy and a book, Make Up: Your Life Guide to Beauty, Style, and Success—online and offline.

Now she's on a mission to do so much more than teach young girls how to wear makeup. She wants to educate women on how to become their entrepreneur and mentor any young creators who want to follow in her footsteps.

(Sawyer and Jarvis 2015)

Are You SoLoMo Ready?

Have you ever searched your name online? What did you find? What could others dig out when they trace your digital footprint? Are you sure you can clean up the digital dirt and avoid the pitfalls? We need to see and treat our name as a brand. The way we develop and maintain our online reputation is crucial for our current and future career. The most important brand you have to protect is "You."

This chapter will discuss the importance of setting up your branding strategy. It is never too early to start doing it. Do not leave it for later. If you wait until you graduate or, even worse, if you become unemployed, it will be too late. Start now! Start building your brand because it takes time and effort. Ask yourself the following question: Am I SoLoMo ready? SoLoMo? The recent growth of connected devices in social networking websites develops a new marketing framework that intersects social media, local, content, and mobile marketing (Papakonstantinidis, Poulis, and Theodoridis 2016).

1. **Social media:** Social networking sites like Facebook, Twitter, and Instagram are proliferating as channels of human communication, allowing brands and consumers to engage in public discussions. As consumers are using social media as their primary source of

information, communication, and entertainment, marketers will be finding a productive environment full of opportunities.

2. **Local and content marketing:** The rapid spread of advanced smartphone and other mobile devices allowed people to exchange information by pinpointing consumers' location and providing them on their mobile devices with location-specific advertisements. The integration of mobile advertising with location-based services is what characterizes location-based advertising.

3. **Mobile devices:** Mobile digital media time has already overtaken desktop and other media Internet access. Smartphone penetration has increased for two reasons. First, wireless networks have become faster and ubiquitous. Second, mobile devices are nowadays more affordable. Mobile marketing can provide consumers with personalized information based on their location and the time of receipt. Consumers are more attached to their phones than their personal computers, providing marketers with new tools and opportunities to attract new customers and develop new markets.

SoLoMo stands out for Social, Local, and Mobile. It is a marketing integration of three interrelated concepts. In today's marketing environment everybody has a voice. Both consumers and brands can talk online. A brand can provide support and advice to people who ask questions on Quora. Products and brands have their social media accounts. For instance, the official match ball of the 2014 World Cup Brazuca was given human characteristics through a creative and anthropomorphic Twitter account. We expect brands to build up a personality. What's the surprise when people behave as brands?

Set Up Your Brand Strategy Early On

Three types of people characterize today's challenging job market: active jobseekers, currently employed, and recruiters. The active job candidates are those who need to find a job immediately. They are either recent graduates or unemployed who seek for quick results and apply to as many available positions as possible. The currently employed or passive jobseekers are those who keep an eye on the job market, without openly signaling their potential interest in new challenges. Finally, many recruiters and job hunters seek for talented employees regardless of their working status.

In any of the three types, personal branding becomes essential. Teri Horton writes in an online post titled Branded for Success that "developing a personal brand ensures that individuals are not left behind and that they develop the competitive advantage that positions them for the career opportunities they deserve." A carefully planned personal brand provides employers with the necessary information for filtering their pool of talents. By developing a unique brand, individuals can use their qualities and skills to market themselves to companies.

Personal branding was always a business tactic for employees to advance within an organization. We apply for promotion by writing down our strengths and unique capabilities. We provide committees with our professional philosophy, vision, and goals to stand out. Social networking websites, such as Facebook, Twitter, Pinterest, and LinkedIn, provide us with the new tools to develop a personal brand that differentiates ourselves from other competitors. We develop a unique personal brand to distinguish from our competitors. A carefully communicated brand is crucial in today's job market since people are looking even when we are not interested. Our name is the most valuable asset in personal branding. As much as we care about what our friends say about us, we should do anything possible to protect our reputation in the digital world.

What steps do we need to follow to set up our branding strategy? What questions should we ask ourselves before going online and communicating our abilities and passions? The next part of this chapter provides some necessary information that seems simple on the surface, but we often overlook it. Let's start with googling ourselves.

Google Yourself

Have you ever *googled* yourself? When was the last time you did? Did you delete the browser's cookies to see what others might find when they type your name into a Google search query? Potential and current employers might be looking as well. Also, your colleagues might be looking for your digital footprint. Even your romantic partner might be curious to know your past by asking Google about it. What will they find about you?

The results of such search query could help recruiters decide whether they want to hire you or someone else. That is the reason why it is more than essential to search for your brand name first. Search for your name in quotes. Try any language you use and compare the results. If people use your common name (i.e., Steve instead of Steven), try typing it as well. Search for all possible results, including images, videos, news, and more. Combine your name with any of your affiliations that include your school, university, neighborhood, summer vacations, and jobs.

Run your search and don't forget to check beyond the first results page. Many times an inappropriate image is hidden in the web, but this does not mean that it does not exist. When I was teaching the course Career Development through Social Media to Honor's students at a university in Greece, I was always asking them to google themselves. Most students used to be shocked and ashamed by the search results. Sometimes we appear on images even when nobody tagged us. We can still control this information using Google's feature to reverse image search. How can you do that? Click the camera icon in the search bar to paste the image URL. Google will search the web and provide us with the link to the website where our image appears even if it does not include our name.

Next, run a search by typing your old and new e-mail addresses and social media usernames. Type your phone numbers and other personal identification information to run a full search. Usually, some forums and websites register users by e-mail addresses, nicknames, and usernames instead of real names. Of course, we should not forget the social networking websites. Run a search of your name and username on social media to check what people write about you or what you have posted in the past that you do not recall.

Finally, use Google Alerts to set up a free personal branding reputation management. Google Alerts is a free service that sends you automated e-mails every time someone mentions your name or any keyword you want. Set up multiple Google Alerts so you will be informed when your name or other personal information appears on the World Wide Web. Knowledge is power, and any information we collect about ourselves and others prepares us better to create our branding strategy.

Removing Unwanted Information

Sometimes we feel helpless when it comes to our online reputation. We think that we can do nothing to protect ourselves from posts and comments that might harm us. That is not accurate though. We should take our digital reputation seriously and work hard to defend it. We should be aware of what we decide to post to our social media accounts from early on. Teenagers should receive proper education to understand the importance of their digital reputation and its consequences for their future. Also, we should know how to remove any personal information we do not wish to be published online, such as the people websites Spokeo and Intelius.

To remove anything unwanted from the Internet, we should start from the search engines. The leader in the category, Google, records by default any search activity such as keywords, images, e-mails, videos, and news. It also marks our location when we use Google Maps or other geo-location services that our smartphones and other connected devices provide. Such services allow the search engines to provide more accurate results to people based on their past searches. Nevertheless, by letting a search engine like Google record every search we do, we are allowing the search engine to store personal information. If we do not want to do that, we can visit the My Account section to check the security and privacy settings to choose what information we want Google to record.

Also, visit the Google Search Help section (2018) "How to remove information from Google." The section posts the following message:

> You can ask Google to remove your sensitive personal information, like your bank account number, or an image of your handwritten signature, or a nude or sexually explicit image or video of you that's been shared without your consent, from Google search results.

Every website and social networking website provides control over the personal information you decide to post online. It takes time to set up your privacy settings, but it pays off in the future. Do not accept anyone to be your friend or connection. Be selective with whom you are connected with on the web.

If unwanted personal information appears on other websites, contact them directly about requesting to remove it. You may refer to the Digital Millennium Copyright Act (1998) Section 512c, which states that "upon receiving proper notification of claimed infringement, the provider must expeditiously take down or block access to the material." If the personal information that appears online is too hard to get off the grid, use reliable privacy protection services (i.e., LifeLock's Privacy Monitor or Abine's DeleteMe) to minimize the damage. Finally, if none of the suggestions helped you remove personal information you do not want to be public, consult a lawyer and report it to the police authorities.

Stories to Get You Hired through Social Media

Social media is affecting everything we know about human communication and business. In Chapter 4 we discussed the concept of social recruiting that contemporary organizations apply to their hiring processes. Job portals like Monster, Indeed, and Simply Hired offer smart solutions to match people with job vacancies; many companies prefer using the power of the social networking websites to cut the liaison. Employers and recruiters search on social media to find out a rare talent or any person who seems to fit their business needs.

Sometimes, these people might not be active jobseekers. They might be college students, entry-level employees, or blue collar workers who post their content using social networking and blogging platforms. These people do not have any intention to get hired or to look for a job. They enjoy socializing online and participating in all sorts of online discussions. They use hashtags and follow online trending topics. There are many stories of people whose online activity got noticed by employers and recruiters. Below are some stories of people who were hired through social media as reported by Claire Landsbaum (2015) in her article "'I Got a Job through Social Media': 5 Millennials Share Their Stories." Landsbaum argues that the impact of social media on the job market is now more evident than before. Recruiters expand their searches to all social networking sites, aiming to find unique talents and passionate professionals. Let's check some of their success stories.

Tracy Clayton, Journalist

Tracy Clayton used her Twitter account to write hilarious comments using the hashtag #BlackBuzzFeed, which became the second most trending topic worldwide. The New York–based Internet media company collected tweets regarding the black version of BuzzFeed. Clayton's original tweets drew a BuzzFeed editor's attention who offered her a job through a direct message. "You never know who's watching you," she said.

Rose McManus, Photographer

The lifestyle blogger Rose McManus increased her popularity through the artistic Instagram account (@rose_mcManus) where she was posting images of coffee mugs and skylines. Her talent in photography attracted followers who started ordering portraits and other photography-related jobs. Her hobby turned out to be her paying job, thanks to Instagram. In her interview with Landsbaum (2015), Rose McManus said,

> Having a brand does not mean establishing a disconnect between you and your account. It means having a distinct understanding of who you are and what you have to offer and effectively communicating that. A brand provides consistency and allows potential customers to anticipate a specific return on their investment.

Celia Ampel, Journalist

A *Miami Herald* intern Celia Ampel started following significant people and decision-makers on Twitter. One of the professionals she followed was *South Florida Business Journal*'s managing editor. Once they had a job vacancy, Celia Ampel received a direct message from the editor asking her if she was interested. As she said, "They were impressed that I was social media savvy." Her main job duties were to maintain the *Business Journal*'s Twitter account, and she seemed the perfect fit for the job. Celia Ampel's advice is to be proactive and interact with the right people on Twitter. "Tweet about your work, but throw in some personal tweets so people can get a sense of who you are. Use common sense and keep them tasteful," she said.

Clark Walker, Barber

Clark Walker used Instagram to follow the account of Fellow Barber. He got connected with the owners and sent pictures of his work. They were impressed by his style and character that made their decision to hire him easy. He took advantage of the professional opportunities Instagram offers and used his account as a digital portfolio to market himself and stand out from the crowd. "Instagram can turn into a great way to show off your portfolio and what types of professional skills you have got, or it can be used to show off your selfies and fancy appetizers. Do what you want with it, just know lots of people might take a look one day," Clark Walker said.

Abigail Carney, Journalist

Abigail Carney applied for a job at Do512, which is an events blog. She was a social media–savvy user, and this is what the blog wanted. Abigail used Twitter for sharing stories and ideas with other people in the media industry. Despite her reservations to work at a young age, she felt that working online and using Twitter was something she loved. In her interview with Landsbaum (2015), Abigail Carney emphasized the importance of being yourself when it comes to personal branding. She responded that

> I'm not necessarily the coolest or most qualified cat, but when responding via Instagram and Twitter I try to use fun and interesting sentences, calling on my copywriting background. Show them some spunk and surprise them—you can do it in 140 characters! Also, make sure your social media account(s) of choice reflect what you're about. I'm a kooky freelance writer who does a myriad of things, so my accounts are goofy stories and pensive, weird photos and ponderings. Know yourself.

Stories to Get You Fired through Social Media

Social media will help you get hired, but misusing it might cause significant trouble to jobseekers. Many times we forget that social media is a public space where almost everyone can check your social media accounts and other personal information that appears online. In what follows, we quote many stories of people who lost their jobs due to social media misuse as found on an article on *People Celebrity* by Lydia Price (2016), which is titled "20 Tales of Employees Who Were Fired because of Social Media Posts."

1. "A former colleague of mine posted about how he was going to use up all his sick leave then quit. He posted it at 9 a.m., and was told he didn't have a job at 11 a.m."

2. "I had to fire someone for this. He was a volunteer firefighter and left for a call which I allowed. Fifteen minutes later someone showed me his five minute-old post of him riding quads saying something along the lines of 'Sometimes you just need to F-off from work.' That put him on a final warning. He then left because he said HIS house was on fire then half-an-hour later his wife tagged him in a photo of him sitting in a kiddie pool in front of his house. The funny thing is, in both cases, if he had simply asked to leave early I probably would have said yes."

3. "I work in a hospital, and there was a police shooting in my area a couple of years ago. Multiple officers were brought into our ER. One officer was DOA, and some hospital employees posted condolences on their Facebook pages with the name of the officer before the family was officially informed. Seven or eight employees were rightfully fired for that one."

4. "I once didn't get a job since I don't have Facebook/etc. Apparently, they wanted to see the kind of person I was, and I told them I like my privacy."

5. "A prospective employee at the company I work for had just passed his interview and was told that all he needs to do is pass a drug test and a physical and he would start on Monday. Someone found the new hire on Facebook and the guy had just posted 20 minutes after the interview, 'S—! Anyone know how to pass a drug test in 24 hours?!'"

6. "I had to fire an employee for a tweet he wrote about a customer. He tweeted '(customer's full name) would be a great name for a porn star.' I found out about it when the customer's lawyer called me the next day threatening action. Turns out the guy worked for the local newspaper and obsessively searched his name on all social media."

7. "I was younger and an idiot. I posted something on Facebook about wanting to go home and play The Sims so I could create a telecommunications store I worked for and then slowly kill off all the customers. I was working a late night shift in a mall and forgot our new coworker had added me on Facebook days before."

8. "I worked in tech assistance at an electronics store in college. A coworker was fired when a famous actor came in, and she posted a lot of his private info on Facebook. Like '[Full name of actor] came into our store and bought this and this and has a black Amex card' and stuff he had on his computer . . . not once but on 2 separate occasions."

9. "One of my Facebook friends worked for the postal service in my town. She posted about how she wanted to kill her boss and went into some gory details. Then, about 5 hours later, she posted another status about how the Feds showed up at her house and that one of her coworkers had shown her boss the status, and she was now fired."

10. "Guy at my company got sacked for putting a racist Facebook status along the lines of 'I hate immigrants' not realizing both his bosses (also owners of the company) were second-generation immigrants from India. They started the company from scratch and now employ 30 people. They pay for full gym membership, health care, and generous pension for all the staff, which he had to say goodbye to when he was fired."

11. "A co-worker of mine was fired recently because he got caught sneaking off from work to smoke and drink. This guy would post photos of him smoking and drinking on Facebook. The boss found out and predictably fired him on the spot. This guy was almost 30-years-old."

12. "A girl I know was a nurse at a hospital and got fired for posting things on Facebook such as: 'Soooooo sleepy here in the ICU. Will someone please code and give me something exciting to do? #isthatbad?' and a lot of racist things. The dumbest part about it was she was TAGGING the hospital she worked at in her posts."

(continued)

13. "Joined a games studio alongside a guy who'd just finished his philosophy degree. He felt that the game's official forums were the best place to discuss whether disabled people would be 'Of as much value as pigs' after a post-apocalyptic event and if they should be simply slaughtered and eaten. All using his company account, of course."

14. "It was my first week on the job a week at a law firm and had to ride with one of the female employees to the UPS store. She was a terrible driver, and almost wrecked multiple times. I posted on Facebook, 'One week on the job and my coworker is trying to kill me; worst driver ever.' The next day I was called into my boss's office with the girl sitting there with an expressionless look on her face, and there was a printout of my post. It was awkward and they fired me on the spot. All of my account information was also set to private, so they figured a way to check my activity."

15. "A few years ago I knew a girl doing social media for a pastry company. Well, this was also around the time of the Casey Anthony trial, and the day the verdict was released she tweeted 'Who's #notguilty about eating all the tasty treats they want?!' It SERIOUSLY blew up and she ended up getting fired a few days later. She was pretty upset about it for a while, but tells the story at parties now and gets that it's pretty funny."

(Price 2016)

Our Brand Ecosystem

Our brand involves many decisions about our style of communication. People understand our brand ecosystem from our level of expertise, our speaking abilities, our technical proficiency, to the clothes we wear, and our room's decoration. Both verbal and nonverbal communication play a major role in how we build and maintain our brand identity. To do so, we need to remember the following:

1. Work on your image: Despite how shallow it might sound, physical appearance matters. It gives people an advantage for making a positive first impression. Do not neglect the way you look. Everything counts.

2. Plan a consistent strategy: You need to have the same look and feel in everything you do and present. Find a name and support it as much as you can. This is your brand name, and you should respect and protect it. Create your hashtag and use it consistently until others start using it as well. Make careful decisions regarding your branded materials (business cards, flyers, websites, social media accounts, and media channels).

3. Familiarize yourself with the camera. Learn how to take good pictures and produce excellent videos. YouTube offers thousands of hours of tutorials to teach you how to buy the right equipment to film like a pro. Also, learn how to make a video resume to communicate your skills to future employers. Most followers get excited with a well-produced video. The days people used to read blog posts are long gone.

4. Build your network: Your professional connections are critical to building and maintaining your brand. This is why it is essential to start branding yourself early on. It takes time to make business connections and associate yourself with key people. It is highly beneficial though.

5. Craft your life's story: Personal branding is not for young talented people who post beautiful pictures and popular videos on social media. Anyone can build a strong brand as long as he/she has a unique story to share.

6. Brand your true self: Never forget to communicate with clarity. People need to identify who you are and what you are offering, which is better than others. Your audience should recognize why you are not the same as the next guy. Focus on what you do best, even if it is the most unusual hobby. Someone is out there ready to listen.

Personal branding enhances your career. There is nothing wrong with communicating your skills and abilities online. As much as we have friends, we now have professional connections that could be useful at any time. Your unique personality is what strengthens the impressions others have about you. In a fast-paced environment where people invent new technologies and applications every day, the future is hard to tell. The final chapter in this book explains the conditions that will shape the brave new online world.

CHAPTER 6

The Brave New Online World

This chapter at a glance:
- Future trends in recruitment
- Recruiting through social media: A recap
- What's next in the brave new world?
- Did this book meet its promises?
- Closing thoughts

Supercar Blondie

Real Name: Alexandra Mary Hirschi
Country: Australia
Social Media: YouTube, Instagram, Facebook
Her story: Alex Hirschi, known as Supercar Blondie, is an Australian social media personality living in Dubai. In March 2018, Arabian Business named her as one of the top 50 most influential women in the Arab world and *Esquire Magazine* Middle East named her as one of the biggest influencers in the region, the only female among her male nominees.

Until April 2017, she cohosted her own talk radio show in Dubai from 4 to 7 p.m.

Alex has interviewed CEOs, politicians, and celebrities such as John Travolta, Jake Gyllenhaal, JC Van Damme, Liam Neeson, and more. On social media, she takes a different approach to traditional car reviews, by creating light-hearted entertainment. She posts regular content on

(continued)

Instagram, Facebook, and YouTube to over 4 million followers. She has also collaborated with BBC's Top Gear and been featured in publications such as Forbes.com, Dailymail.co.uk, Sky News, and Unilad and LadBible. Now, she is a contributor to *Esquire Magazine* ME on cars.

(Supercarblondie.com 2018)

Future Trends in Recruitment

Social media will have a significant role in both job hunting and candidate search in the future. Talent Works International (2017) collected exciting statistics from various research recruitment studies. More specifically, recent research from Jobvite, Hirewell, Jobcast, Captera, and the Recruitment Network Club showed the following:

- As much as 73 percent of social natives found their last job through a social networking website.
- About 67 percent of candidates use Facebook compared to just 35 percent on Twitter.
- About 59 percent of candidates use social media to research companies they are interested in.
- About 48 percent of candidates used social media in the search for their most recent job.
- About 69 percent of active candidates are more likely to apply for a job at a company which manages its employer brand.
- Facebook has more than double the number of active job candidates compared to LinkedIn and Twitter.
- About 83 percent of job candidates are active on Facebook, 40 percent on Twitter, and 36 percent on LinkedIn.
- Job posts get 36 percent more applications if accompanied by a recruiting video.
- About 87 percent of recruiters use LinkedIn, but only 55 percent use Facebook.
- Companies with an integrated approach to talent management have an 87 percent greater ability to hire the best talent.

(Talent Works International 2017)

Of all statistics and findings in the preceding, the last one is the most fascinating. It appears that companies should integrate social media into their talent acquisition strategy without neglecting other recruitment channels. This is because there are excellent candidates who try to maintain their privacy by keeping some distance from social media.

As discussed in Chapter 3, not all millennials contribute to social media. For example, the denials have made a mature decision to protect themselves from the constant social media exposure. Such job candidates should be approached differently if companies want to recruit their talent. Modern recruiters should develop strategies to attract young candidates whether they use social media or not. Hiring managers need to optimize their recruiting strategy by utilizing every contact base with their job candidates. How can we do that?

First of all, we need to know what the job-searching landscape looks like today. Most jobseekers integrate social media into their strategy to search for their next job position. The major social networking websites offer countless opportunities to reach a vast pool of talented employees whether or not they actively seek employment. Nowadays, hiring managers screen candidates' social media accounts to consider them into their final decision.

At the same time, due to the rapid proliferation of online personal branding, young people turn to entrepreneurship by aiming to increase their fan base and online popularity. Not all young graduates are interested in working as employees in a business. They would prefer following the examples of many social media influencers and personas to own profitable social media accounts by displaying their skills and hobbies. A simple online search brings thousands of success stories of people who turned their passion into a profitable business.

Every year more social natives enter the business world. Soon, they will define the majority of the labor market. Recruiters will apply more social media strategies into their recruitment processes. For example, modern HR managers spend time on their company's LinkedIn and Glassdoor accounts to answer questions and reviews. In the so-called war for talent, a carefully crafted social media strategy can attract the most talented employees in each industry and drive profitable results in the future. We should keep an eye on social media trends and learn from leaders and influencers in each sector.

Christine Del Castillo (2016), the former community manager at Workable, suggested that companies should be less antisocial when it comes to social media exposure to attract the best talents. HR managers should emphasize on employer branding and use the digital tools as marketing departments use them for years. Also, Del Castillo (2016) argues that organizations should engage more in smarter social sourcing. Many available online tools such as Boolean Blackbelt and Sourcing Monk offer elaborate and accurate advice on smart sourcing. Companies should never forget that e-mail remains a potent tool to personalize the contact and reach out to candidates in a compelling way.

Recruiters should integrate social media into their hiring strategies, by moving beyond the big three social networks—Facebook, Twitter, and LinkedIn. Nevertheless, in several sectors such as education or programming, other tools are equally or even more critical. For example, in academia, none of the big three social networking websites offers the ultimate solution. Websites such as Research Gate and niche job boards in higher education attract more academics than the popular social media. Also, other sites such as Pinterest, Instagram, and Snapchat have gained their own loyal followers (Jobvite 2018). You don't want to miss them from your search, right?

One-click job applications via social networking websites are becoming a huge trend in social job searching. The mainstream approach to apply through the corporate website seems outdated. Social media–savvy users prefer to send their interest with a click of one button directly via their preferred platforms. For recruiters, every online tool and platform is used to spot the right talent for the job. In their efforts to make their work more time-efficient, recruiters will use job boards that integrate with social networking websites. For example, Workable is an online recruitment software that offers recruiters integrated tools to post jobs, screen candidates, and track applications. As we read on Workable's official website, it suggests recruiters to "source and evaluate candidates, track applicants and collaborate with your hiring teams." Another feature that Workable offers is the Google Chrome extension that enables recruiters to import candidates from social media and streamline their recruiting processes, more accessible than ever.

Gamification in recruitment is another trend that might grow in the future. Many companies see great potential in developing their employer branding once they gamify their hiring processes. Gamification in recruitment is not for all. The previous efforts with the integration of augmented reality tools, such as virtual worlds and games, failed to attract the best talents. Companies tried in the past to set virtual job interviews using online games such as Second Life, but the results were not satisfying.

What about using Big Data in recruiting? Big Data is the collection and analysis of large datasets that allow organizations to make more accurate business decisions based on patterns and insights. Large corporations such as Google and Facebook can benefit from Big Data or People Analytics to not only identify the talents in each industry but also predict their loyalty to the business. Recruiters who use Big Data aim to match a candidate's profile with their organization's unique culture. Neither a typical resume nor a job interview could provide recruiters with such accurate information.

Big Data analysis uses every accessible personal information to scientifically justify new hires. For example, Xerox used Big Data algorithms to recruiting strategies to reduce the turnover rate in its call centers by 20 percent (Martin 2014). Also, Google has developed a retention algorithm to predict the probability of new hires who will make a business impact in the future. Such new technologies and business practices raise ethical concerns regarding their use to make decisions on human lives.

Ethical Considerations

Once people's social media accounts become a substitute for "legal identity," the fine line between unique personal attributes or skills and self-sabotage is blurred. Ethical queries into legal identity and virtual identity are critical both to companies and to job candidates. Deviating too far from moral norms can be perilous. Human resources professionals who use social media to screen candidates are involved in determining ethical and legal factors for internal policy. For job candidates, following guidelines is key to predicting future trends in professional success.

The time is now for social media to act as a catalyst to global labor transitions and social change. Without adequate research on the confidential strategies applied to social recruiting processes, we only have a robust employer branding tool. What is ineffective or harmful during the decision is entirely unrecorded. Ethical use of social media in recruiting schemata is recommended, as the inability to control for high-risk liabilities to a firm during the process may be expensive.

Graduates who have established their career development strategy online now demand clarity, standardization, and performance in their job searches. Upholding the belief that networking is the primary vehicle for professional success, social natives seek to carry the torch of earlier workers as they mobilize social media effectually to their advantage. This is positive reinforcement for software engineering firms and developers involved in deepening the value of social media as a point of leverage for companies invested in optimizing the human resource management (HRM) process. The image-based economy of social media has allowed professionals to sell their capabilities as "identity" in a marketplace of competitor and brand identity exchange.

Online reputation emerges as the last resort. Acknowledgment that confidentiality and expert management of the recruiting process is both ethical and legal is fostered in each electronic contact decision. This is especially so in e-mail and social media interactions to follow mining of recruits and correspondence by those candidates. Each step in the communication process must adhere to ethical guidelines. To ensure integrity in the decision, social recruiting policy updates stand to create consistency between individuals and privacy protections.

Recommendations to Organizations

Experience-based collaboration, networking, and online connectivity create new ways of social interaction. As a result, social recruiting strategies are vital to broader global change management protocol and policy. If a different mentality and patterns of communication are to apply, it is axiomatic that both corporate culture and communication procedures and protocols adapt to this change. Companies need to do more in the area of interfacing human intelligence with artificial intelligence so that creativity turns to profit.

The next generation of employees will seek to enhance their work–life balance. Corporate integration of social media in recruitment and other core functions within the business process value chain allows better initiation of entrepreneurial spirit, and individuated control over their time and activities, as they operate within a network of choices. The future workplace is a manifesto for production. Social natives are likely to backlash against online restrictions while subjecting older generations to technological struggles in the workplace.

For many candidates, emphasis must be on IT and information systems for them to consider future employers. Without this assurance, those candidates may be very reticent about walking through the door of an organization as a full-time employee. Another factor to consider is the trend for younger workers desiring the opportunity of having their creativity and ability to deliver upon it put to trial, although with much more autonomy than would be the case in a standard hierarchy.

Gen Y has grown up "anti-authority," questioning parents, teachers, and even the media they adore. The likelihood of the same attitude toward superiors is high. Hence, the conventional "power" culture, with management firmly in control, maybe one in which stress will develop. Constant feedback and regular and clear statements mirroring IT support sessions are expected. For this reason, social media integration as a communication and HR tool exhibits how organizations are expanding their concept as a partner in business through open-source recruitment measures (i.e., virtual job fairs) and models of tracking employees and other stakeholders.

The subject of generational tension is more profound and deeper than one might perceive; this lack of understanding is due to one's inability to function without multiple devices at hand and an increase in incidents attributable to cultural differences. Firms will have no option but to reevaluate how they go about bringing new staff into the workplace, which is highly likely to involve novel, creative ways of recruitment. The idea that Gen Y workers' expectations about work are not entirely grounded in reality is not without foundation, however. Overinflated sense of worth and faith in technological skill is an ability gone liability, and this leads to unrealistically high expectations of professional advancement on the job.

There is imminent danger that Gen Y will continue to undermine the credibility of older generations on the job if the sole basis of the decision is technological aptitude. A tendency to use technical know-how as the basis for judging others means that Gen Yers might fail to afford other workers sufficient respect. That could apply in particular to managers, who are often older and sometimes lack the technical wizardry of youth. On the other hand, it is possible for the tables to be turned: More experienced staff can be in a comparatively strong position when faced with new colleagues all at sea if company culture does not permit 24/7 access to instant messaging or social networking. The best HRM strategies are already attentive to this problem.

What should we expect in the future? Social networking websites might be used both as recruiting tools and employee referral programs. As jobseekers become more familiar with the use of social networking sites, social hiring is expected to be adopted as a standard process to select potential candidates in the corporate world, especially if those candidates have social referrals from current employees or past employers. With the increase of tools such as Glassdoor, Twitter business pages, Facebook social graph, and LinkedIn company pages, social networks are expected to increase their efforts to shape a more professional character and gain users with specific demographic and psychographic characteristics. However, no one knows whether these certain social networking websites will shape the future of labor market, as technology always changes.

Did This Book Meet Its Promise?

The rules of recruitment and job searching have changed as social natives enter the global workforce. Social natives are now looking for a job in various ways that did not exist five years ago. Emerging technologies, Artificial Intelligence business tools, wearable gadgets, and social media platforms such as LinkedIn, Facebook, BranchOut, Twitter Jobs, Glassdoor, Viadeo, XING, and Bayt, define today's fast-paced professional world. Social Natives use blogs, podcasts, online bios, video résumés, images, selfies, recommendations, and endorsements to publicly demonstrate their skills.

Such online technologies facilitate the recruitment and selection of job candidates via the integration of intelligent software applications in the web-based talent search. The breadth and depth of information increase as HR managers and recruiters embrace new digital tools and platforms. Tomorrow's successful organizations use Big Data, business intelligence, and People Analytics, as well as a plethora of social media screening tools to recruit and retain great talents. When it comes to success in organizations, the wealth of talent offers a precious competitive edge.

This book aims to further the understanding about personal branding and social media recruitment. It also hopes that it inspired the readers through various success stories presented at the beginning of each chapter and other places to take personal branding seriously and view it as vital to their professional career development. Finally, this book examines social nativity as a social phenomenon and presents the latest trends in career development and social recruiting. What is branding and what makes people passionate about it? What is personal branding and how can people develop and maintain a distinct online persona? Who are the current trendsetters in personal branding? Why is social recruiting important? Why is it necessary to set up a personal brand strategy early on? What are some future trends in social recruiting and personal branding? This book provided answers to these questions. Didn't it?

Closing Thoughts

It's clear that social natives struggle to stand out from the crowd. They want to stay ahead and present a positive image that will eventually attract more followers and recruiters. Personal branding is not a one-off job. Our exposure to social media should be constant, clear, and consistent. When Peters (1997) wrote in his manifesto about personal branding, he mentioned the "limitless opportunities for motivated individuals."

Personal branding means you have full control of what you express in public. Sometimes success just happens, but this is an exception, not the rule. Nowadays, too many social media–savvy users plan their strategies carefully and invest time and money to increase their online popularity. You should think of yourself as a brand and be ready for both tremendous love and hate. Not everyone is prepared for personal branding. It requires accepting criticism and bad comments from users who don't really care about your feelings. Your decision to stand out from the crowd is a double-edged sword. It can transform you from an employee who deals with paperwork or waits tables into a leading, independent, and wealthy social influencer.

Peters (1997) predicted the rise of personal branding without having social media in mind. The rapid proliferation of social media boosted the concept that everyone can be a brand. People blog, tweet, buy Google AdWords, post images to Instagram, and create Facebook pages to advance their careers and personal brands. This is our reality in the brave new online world. As more and more people access the same online community platforms, the competition to stand out gets harder. Adding more LinkedIn connections won't matter enough. Eventually everyone will be connected with each other online. Instead, what you say and publish matter. Before you start publishing online, remember that personal branding allows you to

- share your passions and skills;
- demonstrate your strengths and what excites your audience;
- identify your weaknesses and what irritates your audience;
- stand out from your competition;
- build your community, including people who share the same interests;
- establish meaningful communication with others;
- build trust and rapport with others;
- be the most identifiable influencer in your niche;
- not just do things better but also do them differently;
- communicate your messages with clarity, consistency, and constancy;
- boost your confidence and show people what makes you satisfied and happy.

Is personal branding related exclusively to the Internet? The easy answer is yes, but the actual answer is more complicated than it sounds. Dan Schawbel, a personal branding expert and the managing partner of the Gen Y consulting firm "Millennial Branding," argues that overexposure on the Internet might lead to a disastrous burnout of one's brand. The key is the right balance between posting to social media and adding value to people's lives. Personal branding is not only about you. Instead, it is about your audience and what you actually offer them. Whether they want to decide which product is better or how to make a delicate chocolate cake, your branded content should provide solutions.

There is a common misconception that everyone could post anything on social media. Do we really need that? Social media turns many people into mobile journalists who want to record and livestream everything. Nevertheless, not all jobs are branding-friendly. People should define their limits when it comes to posting online content. For example, K–12 teachers should understand the implications of their inappropriate use of social media to protect their young students from online overexposure. Peters (1997) predicted that personal branding will offer the same opportunities to all workers to become famous. In reality, though, branding is still a luxury for those who already have an exciting life.

As Steve Jobs, Apple cofounder and former CEO, used to say at the end of each of his public speeches, "there is one last thing." Many times, the impression we have from someone's well-polished and carefully constructed image is fundamentally fake. Personal branding is about human communication. It isn't about making money and taking advantage of other people's needs and passions. Honesty, credibility, accountability, and integrity are fundamental human values, and the last we want is to encourage more lies and misinformation to our lives.

I would like to end this book with a quote from Ann Friedman (2015), who argued in her article titled "Me, Inc." on the New Republic that

> The more we think of ourselves as brands, the less personal everything becomes. Instead of the real you, with all your quirks and shortcomings, we get a polished YOU, the version that is marketed to the world. Maybe, if you're making a CEO-level salary, the trade-off is worth it. Maybe, if you're naturally outgoing and find yourself in the right industry, it doesn't feel like a trade-off at all. But it seems wrong to extol the virtues of personal branding without at least acknowledging this disconnect. Anything less would be inauthentic.

References

Allen, P. 2011. "Building Your Brand via Social Media." *Sportsturf* 27, no. 9, pp. 20–21.

Anderson, J., and L. Rainie. 2017. *The Future of Truth and Misinformation Online.* Pew Research Center, Retrieved November 21, 2017. http://www.pewinternet.org/2017/10/19/the-future-of-truth-and-misinformation-online

Argenti, P. A. 2007. *Corporate Communication.* New York City, NY: McGraw-Hill, ISBN 9780071254113.

Arruda, W. 2009. "Brand Communication: The Three Cs." *Thunderbird International Business Review* 51, no. 5, pp. 409–16.

Ayres, C. 2017. "The Truth about Dan Bilzerian." *GQ Magazine.* Retrieved November 15, 2017. http://www.gq-magazine.co.uk/article/the-truth-about-dan-bilzerian

Barnett, C. 2010. "Managing Your Personal 'Brand' Online." *Quill* 98, no. 2, pp. 23–32. Retrieved May 2, 2017. http://connection.ebscohost.com/c/articles/49227880/managing-your-personal-brand-online

Boyd, M.D. & Ellison, N.B. 2008. "Social Network Sites: Definition, History, and Scholarship." *Journal of Computer-Mediated Communication, 13,* pp. 210–230.

CareerBuilder. 2017. *Number of Employers Using Social Media to Screen Candidates at All-Time High, Finds Latest CareerBuilder Study.* Retrieved July 2, 2017. http://press.careerbuilder.com/2017-06-15-Number-of-Employers-Using-Social-Media-to-Screen-Candidates-at-All-Time-High-Finds-Latest-CareerBuilder-Study

Chen, C. 2013. "Exploring Personal Branding on YouTube." *Journal of Internet Commerce* 12, 332–47.

Chritton, S. 2013. *Personal Branding and You.* The Huffington Post Blog. Retrieved March 20, 2017. https://www.huffingtonpost.com/susan-chritton/personal-brands_b_2729249.html

Conner, C. 2014. "Use These 5 Tips to Align Employees with Your Brand." *Forbes Online.* Retrieved September 15, 2016. https://www.forbes.com/sites/cherylsnappconner/2014/11/23/use-these-5-tips-to-align-employees-with-your-brand/#49e2843c367d

Deckers, E., and K. Lacy, K. 2012. *Branding Yourself: How to Use Social Media to Invent or Reinvent Yourself.* London, UK: Que Publishing.

Del Castillo, C. 2016. *2016 Social Recruitment Trends Forecast.* Workable Blog. Retrieved May 24, 2018. https://resources.workable.com/blog/2016-social-recruitment-trends-forecast

Dempsey, B. 2017. "Your Brand is More Than a Logo: The Soul of Your Company." *Brandon Dempsey Website.* Retrieved May 12, 2017. https://www.brandon-dempsey.com/your-brand-is-more-than-a-logo-the-soul-of-your-company

Domkundwar, V. 2017. *LinkedIn by the Numbers: 2017 Statistics.* Retrieved May 3, 2017. https://www.readycontacts.com/linkedin-by-the-numbers

Edelman, D. C., and M. Singer. 2015. *Shaping the Digital Customer Journey, Harvard Business Review.* Retrieved November 5, 2016. https://hbr.org/webinar/2015/11/shaping-the-digital-customer-journey

Erskine, P. 2005. *Time Awareness for All Musicians* [Book & CD]. Los Angeles, CA: Alfred Publishing Co., ISBN 13: 978-0-7390-3854-3, 2005.

Erskine, R. 2016. "22 Statistics That Prove the Value of Personal Branding." *Entrepreneur.* Retrieved June 12, 2017. https://www.entrepreneur.com/article/280371

Fill, C. 2005. *Marketing Communications: Engagements, Strategies and Practice,* 4th ed. Essex, UK: Pearson Education Limited/Prentice Hall.

Films Media Group. 2000. *International Branding in the 21st Century [Film].* Performance by Jeff Greenfield, ISBN 978-1-4213-0723-7. Retrieved October 23, 2017. https://ffh.films.com/id/4797/International_Branding_in_the_21st_Century.htm

Forret, M. L., and T. W. Dougherty. 2001. "Correlates of Networking Behavior for Managerial and Professional Employees." *Group & Organization Management* 26, pp. 283–311.

Foulger, M. 2014. "Meet the First Generation of Social Natives." *Hootsuite Blog.* Retrieved June 13, 2017. https://blog.hootsuite.com/social-natives

Friedman, A. 2015. *Me, Inc.: My Paradoxical Quest to Build a Personal Brand.* The New Republic. Retrieved January 5, 2018. https://newrepublic.com/article/122910/my-paradoxical-quest-build-personal-brand

Gandini, A. 2016. "Digital Work: Self-branding and Social Capital in the Freelance Knowledge Economy." *Marketing Theory* 16, no. 1, pp. 123–41.

Gehl, R. W. 2011. "Ladders, Samurai, and Blue Collars: Personal Branding in Web 2.0." *First Monday* 16, no. 5. Retrieved December 9, 2017. http://firstmonday.org/ojs/index.php/fm/article/view/3579/3041

Gibbs, C., F. MacDonald, and K. MacKay. 2015. "Social Media Usage in Hotel Human Resources: Recruitment, Hiring, and Communication." *International Journal of Contemporary Hospitality Management* 27, no. 2, pp. 170–84. doi:10.1108/IJCHM-05-2013-0194

Gibbs, S. 2017. *iPhone X: Thousands Queue as Apple Proves It Still has the X Factor.* Retrieved from https://www.theguardian.com/technology/2017/nov/03/iphone-x-apple-thousands-queue-overnight-fans

Glassdoor for employers. 2017. *Top HR Statistics: The latest stats for HR & Recruiting Pros*. Retrieved March 20, 2017. https://www.glassdoor.com/employers/popular-topics/hr-stats.htm

Gobe, M. 2010. *Emotional Branding; The New Paradigm for Connecting Brands to People*, rev. ed. New York, NY: Allworth Press; updated and revised edition, ISBN 1581156723.

Godin, S. 2009. *Purple Cow, New Edition: Transform Your Business by Being Remarkable*. New York, NY: Portfolio Publishing, ISBN-13: 978-1591843177.

Google Search Help. 2018. *Remove Information from Google*. Retrieved March 2, 2018. https://support.google.com/websearch/troubleshooter/3111061?hl=en

Greer, J. 2010. "The Art of Self-marketing Online: To Find a Job, Enhance Your Social Network and Expand Your Presence on the Web." *US News & World Report*, 147, no. 5, pp. 30–31.

Harris, L., and A. Rae. 2011. "Building a Personal Brand through Social Networking." *Journal of Business Strategy* 32, no. 5, pp. 14–21.

Holmes, F. 2018. "Looking Ahead To $20,000 Bitcoin." *Forbes Online*, Retrieved March 28, 2018. https://www.forbes.com/sites/greatspeculations/2018/03/28/looking-ahead-to-20000-bitcoin/#657b97372ec5

Hooley, T. 2012. How the Internet Changed Career: Framing the Relationship between Career Development and Online Technologies. *Journal of the National Institute for Career Education and Counselling (NICEC)* 29, pp. 3–12.

Horton, T. 2011. "Branded for Success." *TD Magazine* 65, no. 8, p. 72, 2011. https://www.td.org/magazines/td-magazine/branded-for-success

Huxley, A. 1969. *Brave New World*. New York, NY: Harper & Row.

Ingram, M. 2016. *Here's Why Trust in the Media Is at an All-Time Low*. Fortune. Retrieved September 15, 2016. http://fortune.com/2016/09/15/trust-in-media

Internetlivestats.com. 2017. *Google Search Statistics*. Retrieved December 12, 2017. http://www.internetlivestats.com/google-search-statistics

James, C. 2018. *15 People Who Became Rich and Famous Thanks to Social Media*. Retrieved January 13, 2018. https://www.thetalko.com/15-people-who-became-rich-and-famous-thanks-to-social-media

Jobvite. 2016. *Job Seekers Nation Study: Where Job Seekers Stand on the Economy, Job Security, and the Future of Work*. Retrieved March 30, 2018. https://www.jobvite.com/wp-content/uploads/2016/03/Jobvite_Jobseeker_Nation_2016.pdf

Jobvite. 2018. *The New Model for Modern Recruiting: Continuous Candidate Engagement Engage Candidates from First Look to First Day*. Retrieved March 30, 2018. https://www.jobvite.com/wp-content/uploads/2018/01/Jobvite_Continuous_Candidate_Engagement.pdf

Jones, M. 2017. *Why Everyone Needs a Personal Brand (and How To Build Real Influence)*. Inc., Retrieved March 23, 2017. https://www.inc.com/matthew-jones/why-everyone-needs-a-personal-brand-and-how-to-build-real-influence.html

Kaputa, C. 2006. Creating a Brand Strategy. *TD Magazine* 60, no. 4, p. 90.

Khedher, M. 2015. "A Brand for Everyone: Guidelines for Personal Brand Managing." *The Journal of Global Business Issues* 9, no. 1, pp. 19–27.

Kotler, P., and S. J. Levy. 1969. "Broadening the Concept of Marketing." *Journal of Marketing* 33, pp. 10–15. Khedher, M. Dramaturgical Perspective of Online Personal Branding. 2013 World Congress on Computer and Information Technology (WCCIT).

Labrecque, L., E. Markos and G. R. Milne. 2011. "Online Personal Branding: Processes, Challenges and Implications." *Journal of Interactive Marketing* 25, pp. 37–50.

Lair, D. J., K. Sullivan, and G. Cheney. 2005. "Marketization and the Recasting of the Professional Self: The Rhetoric and Ethics of Personal Branding." *Management Communication Quarterly* 18, no. 3, pp. 307–43.

Landsbaum, C. 2015. *"I Got a Job Through Social Media": 5 Millennials Share Their Stories*. LEVO. Retrieved March 2, 2018. https://www.levo.com/posts/i-got-a-job-through-social-media-5-millennials-share-their-stories

Lee, Y-H, and J-Y. Wu. 2013. "The Indirect Effects of Online Social Entertainment and Information Seeking Activities on Reading Literacy." *Computers & Education* 67, pp. 168–77. doi:10.1016/j.compedu.2013.03.001

Lister, M. 2018. *40 Essential Social Media Marketing Statistics for 2018*. WordStream. Retrieved April 18, 2018. https://www.wordstream.com/blog/ws/2017/01/05/social-media-marketing-statistics

Manafu, C. 2004. *Out of love for brands*. Biz Magazine. http://www.saatchikevin.com/wp-content/uploads/2014/06/1062_english_Bizmagazine_Sep04.pdf, (accessed September 3, 2018).

Manafy, M., and H. Gautschi. 2011. *Dancing with Digital Natives: Staying in Step with the Generation That's Transforming the Way Business Is Done*. Medford, OR: Information Today, Inc.

Martin, M. 2014. *Best Uses of Big Data in Recruiting*. Cleverism. Retrieved May 24, 2018. https://www.cleverism.com/best-uses-big-data-recruiting

Meola, A. 2018. *What is the Internet of Things (IoT): Meaning and Definitions*. Retrieved May 18, 2018. http://www.businessinsider.com/internet-of-things-definition

Mitchell, C. 2002. *Selling the Brand Inside*. Harvard Business Review. Retrieved September 21, 2016. https://hbr.org/2002/01/selling-the-brand-inside

Molloy, M. 2017. *Grounded Private Jet for Hire Helps Russians Fake Lavish Lifestyles on Instagram.* Retrieved November 15, 2017. https://www.telegraph.co.uk/news/2017/10/20/grounded-private-jet-hire-helps-russians-fake-lavish-lifestyles

Morton, R. 2012. "Bringing Your Personal Brand to Life." *Healthcare Executive* 27, no. 1, pp. 70–73.

Moses, A. 2009. *Social not-working: Facebook snitches cost jobs.* The Sydney Morning Herald. http://www.smh.com.au/news/technology/web/social-notworking-facebooksnitches-cost-jobs/2009/04/08/1238869963400.html, (accessed Retrieved May 12, 2018).

Panigrahi, D. 2018. "Impact of Social Media on Consumer Entertainment Behaviour: A Paradigm Shift in New Millennium." *Indian Journal of Applied Research* 8, no. 2. Retrieved May 10, 2018. https://wwjournals.com/index.php/ijar/article/view/1546

Papakonstantinidis, S., A. Poulis, and P. Theodoridis. 2016. *R U #SoLoMo ready?: Consumers and Brands in the Digital Era.* New York, NY: Business Expert Press.

Papakonstantinidis, S. 2014. "Social Recruiting: Exploring the Impact of Social Networking Sites on Digital Natives' Occupational Opportunities." *British Library EThOS, EBSCOhost.* Retrieved February 12, 2018. https://lra.le.ac.uk/handle/2381/28623

Papakonstantinidis, S. 2017. "The SoLoMo Customer Journey: A Review and Research Agenda." *Innovative Marketing* 13, no. 4, pp. 47–54, doi:10.21511/im.13(4).2017.05

Parmentier, M., E. Fischer, and A. R. Reuber. 2013. "Positioning Person Brands in Established Organizational Fields." *Journal of the Academy of Marketing Science* 41, pp. 373–87.

Peters, T. 1997. *The Brand Called You.* Fast Company. Retrieved June 18, 2016. https://www.fastcompany.com/28905/brand-called-you

Prensky, M. 2001. "Digital Natives, Digital Immigrants." *On the Horizon* 9, no. 5, pp. 1–6.

Price, L. 2016. *20 Tales of Employees Who Were Fired Because of Social Media Posts.* People Celebrity. Retrieved March 2, 2018. https://people.com/celebrity/employees-who-were-fired-because-of-social-media-posts

Qualman, E. 2009. *Socialomics: How Social Media Transforms the Way We Live and Do Business.* Hoboken, NJ: Wiley and Sons.

Rainie, L., and J. Anderson. 2017. *The Fate of Online Trust in the Next Decade.* Pew Research Center. Retrieved November 21, 2017. http://www.pewinternet.org/2017/08/10/the-fate-of-online-trust-in-the-next-decade

Rampersad, H. 2008. "A New Blueprint for Powerful and Authentic Personal Branding." *Performance Improvement* 47, no. 6, pp. 34–37.

Roberts, K. 2006. *Lovemarks: The Future beyond Brands*. Brooklyn, NY: Power-House Books, U.S.; Revised edition, ISBN-13: 978-1576872703.

Robinette, S., C. Brand, V. Lenz, and D. Hall, Jr. 2000. *Emotion Marketing: The Hallmark Way of Winning Customers for Life*. New York, NY: McGraw-Hill Professional Publishing, ISBN 0071364145.

Roper, S., and C. Fill. 2012. *Corporate Reputation: Brand and Communication*. Essex, UK: Pearson Education Limited.

Sawyer, N., and R. Jarvis. 2015. *YouTube Star Michelle Phan: 7 Things You Didn't Know About Her*. ABC News. Retrieved March 25, 2017. https://abcnews.go.com/Business/youtube-star-michelle-phan-things/story?id=29753510

Schultz, H., and D. J. Yang. 1999. *Pour Your Heart Into It: How Starbucks Built a Company One Cup at a Time*. New York City, NY: Hachette Books, ISBN-13: 9780786883561.

Schawbel, D. 2010. "Branding in a Personal World." *Forbes*, Retrieved June 18, 2016. http://www.forbes.com/sites/danschawbel/2011/01/31/branding-in-a-personal-world/#5af768a91dbd

Shepherd, I. D. H. 2005. "From Cattle and Coke to Charlie: Meeting the Challenge of Self Marketing and Personal Branding." *Journal of Marketing Management* 21, pp. 589–606.

Supercarblondie.com. 2018. *Alexandra Mary Hirschi Personal Website*. Retrieved May 13, 2018. https://supercarblondie.com/about-me-1

Talent Works International. 2017. *8 Social Media Statistics You Need to Know if You're in Recruitment*. Retrieved February 5, 2018. https://www.talent-works.com/2017/09/27/social-media-recruitment

Tapscott, D., and A. Williams. 2008. *Wikinomics: How Mass Collaboration Changes Everything*. London, UK: Portfolio.

The Digital Millennium Copyright Act (DMCA). 1998. U.S. Copyright Office Summary. Retrieved March 2, 2018. https://www.copyright.gov/legislation/dmca.pdf

Van Nuys, A. 2017. Job Seeker Nation Survey: Finding the Fault Lines in the American Workforce, *Jobvite Blog*. Retrieved May 20, 2017. https://www.jobvite.com/jobvite-news-and-reports/2017-job-seeker-nation-survey-finding-fault-lines-american-workforce

Walker, A. 2017. *Unmasked (Episode 1), YouTube Video*. Retrieved February 12, 2018. https://www.youtube.com/watch?v=MQ1xvJI0Qb4

Yeaton, K. 2008. "Recruiting and Managing the 'Why?' Generation: Gen Y." *The CPA Journal*. Retrieved May 7, 2018. http://www.nysscpa.org/printversions/cpaj/2008/408/p68.htm

Yeung, H. W-C. 2009. "Regional Development and the Competitive Dynamics of Global Production Networks: An East Asian Perspective." *Regional Studies* 43, no. 3, pp. 325–51. doi:10.1080/00343400902777059.

YouTube. 2018. *YouTube by the numbers*. You Tube Press Kit. Retrieved February 20, 2018. https://www.youtube.com/yt/about/press

Zur, O., and A. Zur. 2011. "On Digital Immigrants and Digital Natives: How the Digital Divide Affects Families, Educational Institutions, and the Workplace." *Zur Institute - Online Publication*. Retrieved May 16, 2017. http://www.zurinstitute.com/digital_divide.html

About the Author

Stavros Papakonstantinidis is assistant professor at the American University of Middle East in Kuwait, personal branding consultant, and certified corporate trainer. He is an expert in strategic communications with over 15-year work experience in marketing. He received his doctorate in social sciences from the University of Leicester, his MSc in communications from Ithaca College and Cornell University, and his BA in communication and mass media from SUNY New Paltz.

Index

Abine's DeleteMe, 67
Achievers category, 42
ALS Ice Bucket Challenge, 21
Ampel, Celia, 68
Anderson, Janna, 36
Apple, 85

Big Data analysis, 79
Bitcoin, 54
#BlackBuzzFeed, 68
The Body Shop, 9
Boolean Blackbelt, 78
Brand, definition of, 17
Brand identity, definition of, 17
Brand image, definition of, 17
Brand new me, 61–62
    ecosystem, 72–73
    Google yourself, 64–65
    removing unwanted information,
        66–67
    social media
        fired through, 69–72
        hired through, 67–69
    SoLoMo ready, 62–63
    starting strategy early, 63–64
Brand personality, definition of, 17
Brand positioning, definition of, 17
Brand–customer relationship, 5
Branding
    emotional, 7–8
    evolution of, 4–7
    importance of, 2–4
    innovation, four passions of, 8–14
    passionate, 14
Brave new online social world, 53–54,
    75–76
    closing thoughts, 83–85
    ethical considerations, 79–80
    future trends in recruitment, 76–79
    recommendations to organizations,
        80–82

rules of recruitment and job
    searching, 82–83
Brin, Sergey, 34
Brownstein, Alec, 33

Call of Duty (CoD), 52
Carney, Abigail, 69
Castillo, Christine Del, 78
Clayton, Tracy, 68
Content marketing, 63
Contributors category, 41

Deezer, 35
Denials category, 40
Digital jobseekers, taxonomy of,
    40–42
Digital Millennium Copyright Act
    (1998) Section 512c, 67
Digital natives to social natives, 33–37

EDM. *See* Electronic dance music
El Dorado for jobseekers, 54–55
Electronic dance music (EDM), 25
Emotional marketing, 7

Facebook, 6, 21, 23, 26, 62, 64, 78
FIFA, 52
Foulger, Marc, 36
Freelancer.com, 42

Gamification in recruitment,
    58–60, 79
Gen Y, 81–82
Generational tension, 81
Glassdoor, 51, 77
Google, 53
Google AdWords, 33
Google Alerts, 65
Google Chrome extension, 78
Goswami, Manu, 27
GoToMeeting, 52

Grand Theft Auto (GTA), 52
Greve, Gunnar, 25
GTA. *See* Grand Theft Auto
Guru.com, 42

Harlem Shake, 21
Hashtag generation, 32–33
Horton, Teri, 64
HRM. *See* Human resources
    management
Human resources management
    (HRM), 50, 56–57, 80

Idea virus, 10
Instagram, 23, 26, 62
Integrating intelligent software, vii,
    82–83
Internal marketing, 12
Internet, xii, 51, 56
    brief history of, xvi–xviii
Internet of Things (IoT), xiii, 53

Jobs, Steve, 85

King of Instagram, xiv

LifeLock's Privacy Monitor, 67
Lineage, 52
LinkedIn, xix, 26, 50, 64, 77, 78
Livestream, 23
Local marketing, 63
L'Oreal, 60
*Lovemarks—The Future Beyond
    Brands*, 7–8

Marks & Spencer, 6
Marriott International, 59
Mass media world, 19
McManus, Rose, 68
Messina, Chris, 32
Millennial Branding, 84
Mobile digital media, 63
Modern labor market, 24
MSN, 21
Multipoly, 59
My Marriott Hotel game, 59
MySpace, 21

Netflix, 24

Networking, and graduate job
    pursuit, 56–58
New generation, personality traits of,
    38–39
Niche job boards, 78
Nike, 6
NoCopyrightSounds, 25

Odesk.com, 42
Online currency, xiv, 54

Page, Larry, 34
Passion
    for ideas, 9–10
    for life, 10–11
    for people, 11–14
    for values, 8–9
Passionate branding, 14
People Celebrity, 70
People factor, xx
Personal branding, 15, 64, 73, 83
    definition of terms, 17–18
    develop and maintain, 24–26
    era of, xxi–xxii
    evolution of, 18–21
    important, 16–17
    online social entertainment, 21–24
    significance of, xxiii–xxiv
    success of, 27–29
Personal marketing, 3
Pew Internet Center's study, 54
Pinterest, 23, 64
PlayStation, 59
Price, Lydia, 70
PricewaterhouseCoopers (PwC), 59
Procter & Gamble, 4, 7
Purple Cow, 10

Recruiter Nation Survey, 54
Red Bull, 11
Research Gate, 78
Roberts, Kevin, 5
Robinette, Scott, 7
Roddick, Anita, 9

Saatchi & Saatchi, 5
Self-presentation, definition of, 17
Self-promotion, definition of, 17
SimplyHired.com, 56

Skype, 35, 52
Snapchatters, 24
SNS. *See* Social networking sites
Social media, 17, 62–63
    fired through, 69–72
    hired through, 67–69
    hiring process, 51
Social natives, vii
    digital natives to, 33–37
    hashtag generation, 32–33
    and limitless opportunities, 43–47
    recruiting, 38–43
Social networking sites (SNS), vii, 21
Social recruiting, 49, 54
    brave new online social world,
        53–54
    development of, xix–xxi
    El Dorado for jobseekers, 54–55
    gamification in, 58–60
    and its impact on society, 51–52
    networking and graduate job
        pursuit, 56–58
    personal thoughts on, 60
    recruiting 2.0, 50–51
Social screening, 25
Socializers category, 40–41
Sourcing Monk, 78
Spotify, 24, 35
Starbucks, 13–14
Starbucks, 6

Talent Works International, 76
Traditional mass media, 19
20 Tales of Employees Who Were
        Fired because of Social Media
        Posts, 70–72
Twitter, 23, 26, 62, 64, 78

UStream, 23

Vine, 26
Virtual communication channels,
    51–52

Walker, Clark, 69
Wearable Technology, 53
WhatsApp, 35
Wikipedia, 54
Winfrey, Oprah, 20
Wordpress, 26
Workable software, 78
World of Warcraft (WoW), 52
World Wide Web, 34

Xbox, 59
Xerox, 79

YouTube, 22–23, 26, 73

Zuckerberg, Mark, 34

OTHER TITLES IN DIGITAL AND SOCIAL MEDIA MARKETING AND ADVERTISING COLLECTION

Victoria L. Crittenden, Babson College, *Editor*

- *Mobile Commerce: How It Contrasts, Challenges and Enhances Electronic Commerce* by Esther Swilley
- *Email Marketing in a Digital World: The Basics and Beyond* by Richard C. Hanna, Scott D. Swain and Jason Smith
- *R U #SoLoMo Ready?: Consumers and Brands in the Digital Era* by Stavros Papakonstantinidis, Athanasios Poulis and Prokopis Theodoridis
- *Social Media Marketing: Strategies in Utilizing Consumer-Generated Content* by Emi E. Moriuchi
- *Fostering Brand Community Through Social Media* by William F. Humphrey, Jr., Debra A. Laverie and Shannon B. Rinaldo
- *#Share: How to Mobilize Social Word of Mouth (sWOM)* by Natalie T. Wood and Caroline K. Muñoz
- *The Seven Principles of Digital Business Strategy* by Niall McKeown and Mark Durkin
- *Digital Branding Fever* by Athanasios Poulis, Ioannis Rizomyliotis, and Kleopatra Konstantoulaki
- *M-Powering Marketing in a Mobile World* by Syagnik Banerjee, Ruby Roy Dholakia and Nikhilesh Dholakia

Announcing the Business Expert Press Digital Library

Concise e-books business students need for classroom and research

This book can also be purchased in an e-book collection by your library as

- *a one-time purchase,*
- *that is owned forever,*
- *allows for simultaneous readers,*
- *has no restrictions on printing, and*
- *can be downloaded as PDFs from within the library community.*

Our digital library collections are a great solution to beat the rising cost of textbooks. E-books can be loaded into their course management systems or onto students' e-book readers. The **Business Expert Press** digital libraries are very affordable, with no obligation to buy in future years. For more information, please visit **www.businessexpertpress.com/librarians**. To set up a trial in the United States, please email **sales@businessexpertpress.com**.